Cycling the Palm Springs Region

D0974894

Cycling the Palm Springs Region

By Nelson Copp

CARTOGRAPHER
Margaret Gooding

Sunbelt Publications
San Diego, California

Cycling the Palm Springs Region

Sunbelt Publications, Inc
Copyright © 2009 by Nelson Copp
All rights reserved. First edition 2009, second printing 2013

Cartography by Margaret Gooding
Cover and book design by Kelly Johnson
Project management by Deborah Young
Printed in the United States of America

Sunbelt Publications, Inc.
P.O. Box 191126 San Diego, CA 92159-1126
(619) 258-4911, fax: (619) 258-4916
www.sunbeltbooks.com

"Adventures in the Natural History and Cultural Heritage of the Californias"
A Series Edited by Lowell Lindsay

16 15 14 13   5 4 3 2

Library of Congress Cataloging-in-Publication Data

Copp, Nelson. Cycling the Palm Springs region / by Nelson Copp ; cartographer, Margaret Gooding. -- 1st ed.
p. cm. Includes bibliographical references and index. ISBN 978-0-932653-93-2
1. Bicycle touring--California--Palm Springs--Guidebooks. 2. Palm Springs (Calif.)--Guidebooks. I. Title. GV1045.5.C22P364 2009 796.6'40979497--dc22
2008053696

All photographs by the author unless noted.

CONTENTS

Indicates a mountain bike ride

ACKNOWLEDGMENTS

The Desert Bicycle Club, a recreational cycling club, for promoting cycling activities in the Coachella Valley and for inspiring and providing feedback for several rides in the book. *http://www.cycleclub.com*

Jim Foote, Monument Manager, Santa Rosa and San Jacinto Mountains National Monument, for his dedication in helping the Coachella Valley Multiple Species Habitat Conservation Plan come to fruition and for providing valuable feedback on a number of rides in the book that showcase this beautiful National Monument.

INTRODUCTION

DESCRIPTION AND HISTORY

Palm Springs has long been a mecca for the rich and famous, including movie stars looking for a place to relax and escape from media scrutiny, and people longing for the warm desert clime. In the 1930s and 1940s many movie stars bought second homes in the area. But long before Palm Springs was "discovered" by the rich and famous the valley was a winter home for Native Americans who migrated from the surrounding mountains to the warmer desert floor and palm oases during the winter. They also frequented the mineral springs and many cool canyons in the area including Palm, Andreas, and Murray canyons. Water and food was readily available, enabling them to grow crops and flourish.

The Agua Caliente Band of Cahuilla Indians inhabited and governed around 2000 square miles of land in the area. The Federal Government gave the odd-numbered sections of the land to the Southern Pacific Railroad in the 1860s and created the Agua Caliente Indian Reservation from the even-numbered sections in 1876. The tribe maintains primary control of much of the land in Palm Springs, Cathedral City, Rancho Mirage and other unincorporated areas including important desert and mountain habitat. The Agua Caliente Band of Cahuilla Indians developed a Tribal Habitat Conservation Plan to identify plants, animals, and habitat that must be preserved or protected, including the habitat for the Peninsular bighorn sheep.

Settlers began moving to the valley after the 1885 act that provided land to homesteaders. The Homestead Trail, part of the Cahuilla Hills "Cowboy" Trails ride, was named after these settlers. In the late 1800s the Southern Pacific Railroad established the "Indian Wells" distribution point in the eastern part of the valley and the first date palm shoots were imported from Algeria. The name of the town was changed to Indio in 1879. By 1920 Indio had become the date capital of the United States. The Indio Mural Tour ride visits a number of murals depicting much of the history of the Coachella Valley. Indio became the Coachella Valley's first incorporated city in 1930 and the All-American Canal began delivering much needed Colorado River water in 1948.

In the western part of the valley the Palm Springs Hotel opened in 1887 near Tahquitz Canyon Way and Palm Canyon Drive close to the popular hot springs. Other famous hotels began to draw celebrities and famous people. A number of interesting neighborhoods followed soon including the Movie Colony, Old Las Palmas, Deepwell, and Tennis Club to name a few. The Deepwell Tour, Canyon Country Club Route, and the two Palm Springs City Loop rides wind their way through these and many more beautiful neighborhoods.

During World War II General Patton took up residence in the Hotel Indio and trained his troops nearby. The Box Canyon Earthquake Route ride starts near the General George S. Patton Museum at Chiriaco Summit.

After the war Palm Springs was no longer a secret and development quickly spread throughout the valley. Now the Coachella Valley consists of a number of cities from west to east including Palm Springs, Cathedral City, Rancho Mirage, Palm Desert, Indian Wells, La Quinta, Indio, and Coachella. The area is known for its hot springs, championship golf courses, and exclusive resorts and is a winter getaway for many tourists.

The many rides in this book travel through the various cities and showcase the majestic vistas of the San Jacinto and Santa Rosa Mountains and the sublime weather—both ideal for bicycling.

CLIMATE

The Palm Springs Region is bounded on the north by the Little San Bernardino Mountains, on the south by the Santa Rosa Mountains, and on the west by the San Jacinto Mountains and the towering 10,000-foot Mount San Jacinto. These mountains block moisture creating a rain-shadow effect that limits rainfall to less than 6 inches annually and creates the famous warm, dry climate. Winter temperatures are a comfortable 70s by day and 40s at night. Summer temperatures quite often climb above 100 with temperatures in the nearby mountains 25-30 degrees cooler; a number of mountain rides in the book can provide a welcome escape from the heat.

TOPOGRAPHY

The Coachella Valley is located within the Colorado Desert, which is the western extension of the larger Sonoran Desert that extends across the southwest U.S. and northwest Mexico. The elevation is generally below 1000 feet and actually below sea level in the Salton Sea area.

The San Andreas Fault zone begins southeast of the Salton Sea and runs northward through the Coachella Valley along the base of the San Bernardino Mountains and for 600 miles to northwest California. The fault zone is a two-to eight-mile-wide region of intensely twisted and folded landscape, a result of horizontal shifting of tectonic plates and action along the fault where opposite sides of the fault slide past one another at a couple of inches a year. You can experience some of this amazing landscape by riding the Box Canyon Earthquake Route ride or the Painted Canyon ride that head through the Mecca Hills, an artist palette of colorful badlands of uplifted, twisted and folded sedimentary rocks and narrow canyons. Or enjoy the Coachella Valley Preserve and Dillon Road Ride where you pass by the nearly vertical tilted Indio Hills. Many of the maps in the book indicate the location of various faults.

FLORA AND FAUNA

The Palm Springs region has an amazing diversity of plant and animal life from the desert floor to the nearby mountains. Typical vegetation you might find on your rides is creosote bush, yucca and cholla cactus, saltbush, smoketree, palo verde trees, and pinyon pine, California juniper, manzanita, and Coulter pine at higher elevations. A large percentage of the plant species are annual spring grasses and wildflowers brought on by the winter rains. Much of the wildlife in the region is focused around runoff from seasonal rains, springs, and fan palm oases. If you're lucky you might encounter mule deer, jackrabbits, desert tortoise, Gambel's quail, and the greater roadrunner. The endangered Peninsular bighorn sheep frequents the hillsides in the region but is difficult to spot and should be avoided if seen.

SANTA ROSA AND SAN JACINTO MOUNTAINS NATIONAL MONUMENT

The Santa Rosa and San Jacinto Mountains rise from the desert floor creating a spectacular backdrop to the many Coachella Valley communities. The National Monument provides a wonderful backcountry destination to experience wildlife, desert and mountain vegetation, and plenty of open space that can be accessed from a number of multiuse trails.

The Santa Rosa and San Jacinto Mountains National Monument was established by an Act of Congress on October 24, 2000 "in order to preserve the nationally significant biological, cultural, recreational, geological, educational, and scientific values found in the Santa Rosa and San Jacinto Mountains and to secure now and for future generations the opportunity to experience and enjoy the magnificent vistas, wildlife, land forms, and natural and cultural resources in these mountains and to recreate therein."

The cities of Cathedral City, Coachella, Indian Wells, Indio, La Quinta, Palm Desert, Palm Springs, and Rancho Mirage, along with the County of Riverside, Coachella Valley Water District, and Imperial Irrigation District have signed the Coachella Valley Multiple Species Habitat Conservation Plan (CVMSHCP). The plan permanently conserves 240,000 acres of open space and protects 27 threatened plant and animal species across the Coachella Valley and in the Santa Rosa and San Jacinto Mountains National Monument. The plan preserves the Coachella Valley's native desert wildlife and creates a magnificent system of open space parks, trails, and reserves. In addition it safeguards significant wild-life habitat linkages and wildlife corridors.

A research program is underway to evaluate the effects of recreational trail use on Peninsular bighorn sheep within essential habitat in the Santa Rosa and San Jacinto Mountains. The research will address the response of bighorn sheep to recreational use of trails in these areas and possibly change the usage level of some trails in the future. To monitor trail use some trails will be subject to a self-issue permit system that will be designed to be friendly and will not be limited in number. These may be available at kiosks at the trailhead or online and is not fully defined yet. Failure to have a permit in possession when using these trails may result in a citation. Rides in this book that are currently affected by this are the Art Smith Trail west of its intersection of the Hopalong Cassidy Trail and two possible optional extended portions of that trail on the Hahn Buena Vista Trail and the Cathedral Canyon Trail. Also affected is the Bear Creek Canyon Trail south of Bear Creek Oasis and the Boo Hoof Trail south of that area in the Cove Oasis Trails ride. In addition, these sections of the trails are closed to recreation-al activity during the hot season from June 15 through September 30. Refer to these ride descriptions for more specific information.

Why should you respect these trail limitations? With the large number of people enjoying recreational activities of various kinds a balance must be maintained between enjoying our natural surroundings and preserving them for current and future generations. Unlimited use of outdoor areas is just not feasible any more. In order to continue using the trails we must all abide by these guidelines.

USING THIS BOOK

Each of the trips in this book follows a consistent format and are arranged by region. West Valley rides are mainly in the Palm Springs and Cathedral City areas. Central Valley rides are in the Rancho Mirage, Palm Desert, and Indian Wells areas. East Valley includes La Quinta, Indio, Coachella, and the Mecca region. The Mountain rides are in the San Jacinto, Santa Rosa, and San Bernardino Mountain areas.

Use the area map of the Palm Springs region on the inside front cover to find the general area in which you are interested in riding. Select several ride choices and then use the detailed map and description in each ride to narrow down the location and gather detailed information about the rides. Appendix 1 lists the rides by difficulty.

The beginning of each ride includes a summary of information to help you select rides and to plan for them. The end of each ride describes additional useful information about each ride, including how to get to the starting point, any amenities nearby (including food, water). Links to useful web sites and nearby bike shops can be found in the Coachella Valley Cyclist's Directory in Appendix 3.

Starting Point: Specific location and city of the starting point of the ride.

Distance: Length of the entire ride in miles as described in the text and plotted on the accompanying trip map and elevation profile. Distance does not include any optional routes unless otherwise indicated. Most rides are round-trip unless noted as out and back indicating the return route is the same as the initial route. A few rides are indicated as one-way indicating they are usually ridden only in one direction and may require a car shuttle. Cumulative mileages are described in the text of many rides so it is useful to have a bike computer to keep track of where you are in relationship to the write-up. Mountain bike rides that combine both paved and dirt roads will indicate the distance of each.

Elevation Gain/Loss: Total vertical elevation gain and loss (sum) for the whole route unless indicated as one way in which case just reverse the numbers for the return route. Steeper rides generally include an average percent grade to help you understand the trail or road steepness as it rises and falls along its route. Percent grade is calculated as the height increase divided by the horizontal distance. 4% to 5% grade could be considered moderate while 6% to 8% more strenuous and 9%+ difficult. If the grade is steep only in a few spots those can be easily walked. Elevation contour maps are provided for trips with significant elevation change.

Riding Time: An estimate based on 12 MPH average speed for road bike rides and roughly 4 MPH average speed for mountain bike rides. Keep in mind that these are only estimates. Fast riders may be able to complete the trip in half the time while leisurely riders may take more time than stated.

Difficulty: Rating of how hard the ride is with consideration for elevation gain, trip distance, and condition of the route and difficulty is based on what a reasonably fit rider is capable of doing. Both a difficulty level and a technical rating are provided. The difficulty ratings are *easy, moderate, difficult* and *strenuous* with difficult and strenuous based on longer distance or higher elevation gain. The technical ratings are *not technical, technical in spots*, and *technical* indicating how hard the route is to negotiate with narrow single track, rocky sections, or precipitous exposure the primary reason for more technical ratings. Note that trail conditions can change and it is a good idea to check with bike shops or local web sites regarding the latest trail conditions.

Road Conditions: The type of surface you will ride on. The conditions are *city streets* for most road rides and *dirt roads* and *trails* for most mountain bike rides. Mountain bike rides that combine both paved and dirt roads will indicate the distance of each.

Season: The best time of the year to ride a route. Desert temperatures can change dramatically so it is a good idea to start early during the warmer months to avoid afternoon high temperatures. Rides in the mountains can be warm in the summer but you may also encounter snow in the winter months. It is always a good idea to check local weather sites to prepare for your rides.

Equipment: The type of bicycle needed for the ride. *Any bicycle* (if well maintained) can be used for most road rides while *mountain bikes* are required for most mountain bike rides.

Optional Topo Map: Each ride has an accompanying detailed bike map. A summary of symbols and features used in those maps is provided in the GPS and Maps section. In addition to the detailed maps you may also want to consider taking along a topographic map with more detailed topography information. The name of the USGS topographic map for the ride is listed here.

GPS AND MAPS

The mountain bike routes on the maps in this book were created by riding the trails using a handheld Global Positioning System (GPS) receiver. The starting point of each ride and a few other key points on the detailed maps are shown with the Universal Transverse Mercator (UTM) coordinate of that position. You can enter this in your GPS to help find the point or in case you get turned around, to find your way back to the starting point. If you carry a GPS, which is highly recommended for mountain bike rides, you should always save the ride starting point as a safety precaution.

To set up your GPS to match the maps and UTM locations the datum, which is a reference surface for the map, should be set to North American Datum of 1927. The units should be set to UTM/UPS (not longitude and latitude).

MAP SYMBOLS AND FEATURES

Master Legend

⊶⊶⊶	Bike Trail/Route	⟲	Folded Rocks	⊹	Road Junction
⊓	Billers Bailout sign	⬗	Ladder Canyon Hike	🌴	Palm Oasis
)(	Bridge	Ⓐ	Campground		
⊓	Drinking Fountain	●━●	Gate	⊞	View Point
⊓	C.V. Museum	STOP	Not Authorized	⊖	Water Tank
⊡	Mural	⊞	Park	⊖	Wash
⊷	Cross golf cart road	P	Parking	——	Roadway
⊓	Cross on top of hill			—·—··	Stream
⊕	Rocky Area	◎	Spring	-----	Canal
•••	Top of Switchbacks	⬆	Start	—··	Earthquake Faults
		⌂	Visitor Center	⬡	Lakes
				▭	National Parks and Monuments

SOURCES FOR MAPS

- DEM/Hillshades: National Elevation Data (USGS)
- Streams: National Hydrography Dataset (USGS, EPA, US Forest Service)
- Faults: California Geological Survey (2005)
- Roads and Cities: County of Riverside (2006)
- Major roads (inset map): BLM
- National Parks, Monuments, Preserves: BLM, USGS
- Lakes (inset map): State of California

SPECIAL OFF-ROAD PREPARATION

Whether you're riding on trails near town or in the backcountry, a few precautions should be taken to ensure your safety and the integrity of your equipment. Mountain bike riding can be a dangerous sport for both you and your equipment and now and then you will fall off your bike or will have equipment failures. Always carry plenty of food, water, a knife, and a first aid kit with basic items to help with scrapes and cuts. A comb or tweezers are useful for extracting cholla balls or other cactus spines. A map and compass are advised for routes where the city will not always be in sight and a light for longer or late afternoon rides. Sunglasses and sunscreen are especially important during warmer months and remember that higher elevations provide more exposure to the sun's harmful rays. Sun protective clothing is the best choice to prevent over-exposure to the sun.

Always ride with several friends and try to stay together. If someone gets hurt or has a major equipment failure, one or more people can stay behind and others can go for help. Cell phones work in some places but do not rely solely on them. Also, do not rely on your friends to carry your extra equipment, food, or water. Carry more that what you think you will need in case you get separated or your friend is relying on you. Tell someone at home where you will be riding and when you will return in case you do not return when expected.

Before you leave home always check your tires, chain (make sure it is lubed), brakes, and shifting mechanism to make sure they are in good working order. A tune-up at a bike shop is recommended if you have not ridden your bicycle in awhile. You should carry at least the following equipment with you:

- 1-2 spare inner tubes (more for rides with lots of cacti or use a slime product in your tubes)
- Patch kit (make sure the glue is still good)
- Tire pump (test it beforehand)

- Tire levers
- Allen wrenches of varying sizes to fit your bike
- Multipurpose or all-in-one type tool
- Spoke wrench that fits your spokes
- Chain tool (some all-in-one tools include this)
- First aid kit
- Map and compass
- GPS and extra batteries (not a substitute for a compass and map)
- Knife
- Extra food
- Water—several liters, more for long rides
- Comb or tweezers for cactus
- Light
- Sunscreen
- Sunglasses
- Windbreaker for longer or afternoon rides

RESPONSIBLE RIDING

Many health-conscious people are enjoying bicycle riding as a popular way to exercise and to enjoy the outdoors. As energy costs soar, people are also looking for alternative means of transportation, like bicycling. As a result, more people are bicycling on and off the road and it becomes more important for everyone to follow basic guidelines to increase safety and enjoyment and to prevent trails from becoming off limits to bicycles.

As a bicyclist you must follow traffic laws, including stopping at stop signs and red lights and riding in the same direction as traffic. Always position yourself where motorists can see you. Many bicycle accidents occur when riders do things motorists are not expecting. Always signal your intentions and you will have a more enjoyable and safe ride.

The Palm Springs region has a number of wonderful trails and when riding off-road there is a certain level of responsibility you must assume as a trail user. You will share most trails with hikers and equestrians and in both cases you must yield the right of way. The International Mountain Bicycling Association (IMBA) has a set of Rules of the Trail that should be followed to ensure safe and enjoyable use of the trails. If you are already following these rules you are going a long way towards safe and courteous riding on shared-use trails.

INTERNATIONAL MOUNTAIN BICYCLING ASSOCIATION (IMBA) RULES OF THE TRAIL

These guidelines for trail behavior are recognized around the world. IMBA developed the "Rules of the Trail" to promote responsible and courteous conduct on shared-use trails. Keep in mind that conventions for yielding and passing may vary, depending on traffic conditions and the intended use of the trail.

1. RIDE ON OPEN TRAILS ONLY

Respect trail and road closures—ask a land manager for clarification if you are uncertain about the status of a trail. Do not trespass on private land. Obtain permits or other authorization as may be required. Be aware that bicycles are not permitted in areas protected as state or federal Wilderness.

2. LEAVE NO TRACE

Be sensitive to the dirt beneath you. Wet and muddy trails are more vulnerable to damage than dry ones. When the trail is soft, consider other riding options. This also means staying on existing trails and not creating new ones. Don't cut switchbacks. Be sure to pack out at least as much as you pack in.

3. CONTROL YOUR BICYCLE

Inattention for even a moment could put yourself and others at risk. Obey all bicycle speed regulations and recommendations, and ride within your limits.

4. YIELD TO OTHERS

Do your utmost to let your fellow trail users know you're coming—a friendly greeting or bell ring are good methods. Try to anticipate other trail users as you ride around corners. Bicyclists should yield to all other trail users, unless the trail is clearly signed for bike-only travel. Bicyclists traveling downhill should yield to ones headed uphill, unless the trail is clearly signed for one-way or downhill-only traffic. Strive to make each pass a safe and courteous one.

5. NEVER SCARE ANIMALS

Animals are easily startled by an unannounced approach, a sudden movement or a loud noise. Give animals enough room and time to adjust to you. When passing horses, use special care and follow directions from the horseback riders (ask if uncertain). Running cattle and disturbing wildlife are serious offenses.

6. PLAN AHEAD

Know your equipment, your ability and the area in which you are riding—and prepare accordingly. Strive to be self-sufficient: keep your equipment in good repair and carry necessary supplies for changes in weather or other conditions. Always wear a helmet and appropriate safety gear.

http://www.imba.com/

Trip W1 - Tram Road Ride

Starting Point	North Palm Springs
Distance	8 miles out and back
Elevation Gain/Loss	2150'/2150'
Riding Time	90 minutes or more depending on your aerobic shape
Difficulty	Difficult, not technical, 9.6% grade hill climb
Road Conditions	City street
Season	Fall, Winter, Spring
Equipment	Any bicycle
Optional Topo Map	Palm Springs, CA

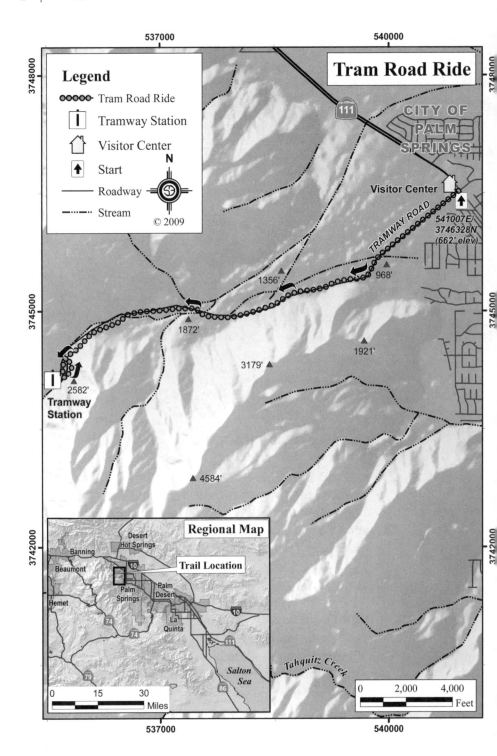

Tram Road Ride

Legend

- ●●●●● Tram Road Ride
- [↑] Tramway Station
- ⌂ Visitor Center
- ↑ Start
- ─── Roadway
- ·──·──· Stream

© 2009

N

CITY OF PALM SPRINGS

Visitor Center

TRAMWAY ROAD

541007E/
3746328N
(662' elev)

1356' ▲

968' ▲

1872' ▲

1921' ▲

3179' ▲

[I] Tramway Station

2582' ▲

4584' ▲

Regional Map

Desert Hot Springs

Banning

Beaumont

10

Palm Springs

Palm Desert

Hemet

74

La Quinta

74

111

79

Salton Sea

86

Trail Location

Tahquitz Creek

0   15   30
Miles

0   2,000   4,000
Feet

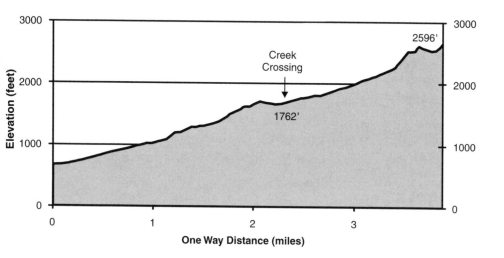

Even though the road to the Palm Springs Aerial Tramway is only 4 miles in length, it packs a punch, since it gains 2150 feet with an average grade of 9.6%. Many cyclists, runners, and hikers do the route as a great morning training workout.

The tramway was built in rugged Chino Canyon, which provided quite an engineering challenge at the time. Construction started in the early 1960s and helicopters were used to build four of the five towers. The tramway was dubbed by some as the eighth wonder of the world. In 2001 the original cars were replaced by ones that rotate, providing a 360 degree view on the way up. The 10-minute ride carries passengers from the Valley Station at 2643 feet to the Mountain Station at 8516 feet. The temperature can be 30 degrees cooler at the top. Note that bikes are not allowed on the tramway.

The ride starts near the Palm Springs Visitor Center, described as a "Googie-style" or desert modern building. Designed as a gas station by Albert Frey and Robson Chambers, it was completed in 1965. In 2002 Palm Springs saved it from demolition by purchasing it and converting it into a visitor center.

Start pedaling west on Tramway Road. The road maintains a steady 9.6% grade as you start heading up the alluvial fan of Chino Canyon. In less than a mile the road curves to the left and brings you closer to the Santa Rosa Mountains on your left. When the gravel levee on your right joins the Tramway Road, the canyon begins to narrow a bit more.

Around 2.5 miles you cross a small bridge and a small creek below. Continue climbing and soon you reach the lower parking lots. As you reach the tramway station, stay to the right and follow the road past the station. As it curves left it starts dropping and rejoins the main road. Begin your fast descent back to the starting point, watching out for runners and hikers.

GETTING THERE

Take North Palm Canyon Drive to Tramway Road and park in this area.

AMENITIES

Water and restrooms are available at the visitor center and the tramway station.

Trip W2 - Palm Springs City Loop

Starting Point	Downtown Palm Springs
Distance	2.5 miles
Elevation Gain/Loss	50'/50'
Riding Time	30 minutes
Difficulty	Easy, not technical
Road Conditions	City streets
Season	Fall, Winter, Spring
Equipment	Any bicycle
Optional Topo Map	Palm Springs, CA

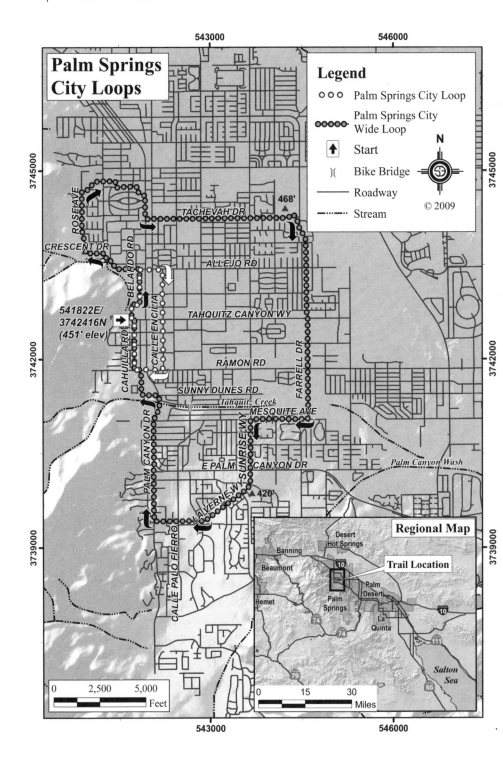

Palm Springs
City Loops

Legend

∘∘∘ Palm Springs City Loop

⊙⊙⊙⊙⊙ Palm Springs City
Wide Loop

↑ Start

)(Bike Bridge

—— Roadway

—··—··— Stream

N

© 2009

ROSE AVE

CRESCENT DR

BELARDO RD

TACHEVAH DR

468'

ALLEJO RD

541822E/
3742416N
(451' elev)

CALLE ENCILIA

CAHUILLA RD

TAHQUITZ CANYON WY

RAMON RD

SUNNY DUNES RD

Tahquitz Creek

MESQUITE AVE

FARRELL DR

PALM CANYON DR

SUNRISE WY

E PALM CANYON DR

Palm Canyon Wash

LA VERNE WY

420'

CALLE PALO FIERRO

Regional Map

Desert
Hot Springs

Banning

Beaumont

10

Trail Location

Palm
Desert

Hemet

Palm
Springs

La
Quinta

10

74

74

111

79

Salton
Sea

86

0   2,500   5,000
Feet

0   15   30
Miles

Palm Springs draws visitors from all over the world to its warm climate, wonderful landscape, and many activities. It is a very bike-friendly town with many signed and striped bike routes. This ride follows the Palm Springs Downtown Loop bike route. It is a great introduction to the heart of downtown Palm Springs with nearby access to popular stores and restaurants in the area.

Head west on Ramon Road and turn right on Cahuilla Road. Watch the speed humps on this street. This area is called Tennis Club. Turn left on Tahquitz Canyon Way and then veer right on Museum Road and continue past the Palm Springs Desert Museum at 101 Museum Drive. This architecturally innovative building is striking and almost blends into the hillside. It is both an art museum and a natural and local history museum.

Follow Museum Drive as it curves right then left past Desert Fashion Plaza and becomes Belardo Road. Turn right on Alejo Road and cross North Palm Canyon Drive and then North Indian Canyon Drive. The Movie Colony area is on your left, named after all the stars and directors that have owned property there.

Turn right on North Calle Encilia. You pass by the Spa Desert Casino, which actually takes up several blocks. Turn right on North Ramon Road and pass by the Warm Sands area on your left as you pedal back to your starting point.

OPTIONS

If you are interested in the movie stars that lived and played in Palm Springs, the Walk of Stars is along the sidewalk on South and North Palm Canyon Drive between Alejo Road and Baristo Road. The stars of Rudolph Valentino, Shirley Temple, Clark Gable, Frank Sinatra and many others are found here. You must walk your bike on the sidewalk but it might be an interesting post-ride activity. Walk of Stars Brochures are available, marking the location of the various stars.

GETTING THERE

The ride can start anywhere on the loop but parking is readily available near the intersection of Ramon Road and Belardo Road. From South Palm Canyon Drive turn west on Ramon Road to Belardo Road and park here.

AMENITIES

Plenty of restaurants are available in this area for post ride nourishment.

Trip W3 - Palm Springs City Wide Loop

Starting Point	Downtown Palm Springs
Distance	11 miles
Elevation Gain/Loss	250'/250'
Riding Time	1 hour
Difficulty	Easy, not technical
Road Conditions	City streets
Season	Fall, Winter, Spring
Equipment	Any bicycle
Optional Topo Map	Palm Springs, CA

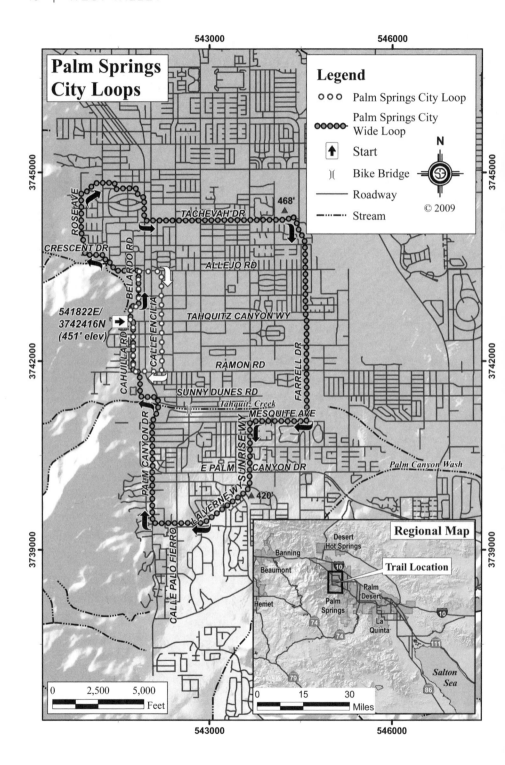

Palm Springs City Loops

Legend

○ ○ ○ Palm Springs City Loop

○○○○○ Palm Springs City Wide Loop

⬆ Start

)(Bike Bridge

—— Roadway

–··–··– Stream

© 2009

N

Regional Map

Trail Location

Desert Hot Springs

Banning

Beaumont

Palm Desert

Hemet

Palm Springs

La Quinta

Salton Sea

0   15   30
Miles

0   2,500   5,000
Feet

541822E/
3742416N
(451' elev)

ROSE AVE

CRESCENT DR

BELARDO RD

CAHUILLA RD

CALLE ENCILIA

PALM CANYON DR

CALLE PALO FIERRO

LAVERNE WY

SUNRISE WY

TACHEVAH DR

ALLEJO RD

TAHQUITZ CANYON WY

RAMON RD

SUNNY DUNES RD

Tahquitz Creek

MESQUITE AVE

E PALM CANYON DR

FARRELL DR

Palm Canyon Wash

468'

420'

Palm Springs has long been a mecca for the rich and famous including actors, politicians, and entertainers looking for a place to relax and escape from media scrutiny. In the 1930s and 1940s many movie stars bought second homes in the area. Interesting neighborhoods in Palm Springs include The Movie Colony named after all the stars and directors that have owned property there, Old Las Palmas with large estates, Deepwell (built in the 50s and 60s) with lush landscaping and palm trees, and Tennis Club with nice private residences. This ride winds its way through these and many more beautiful neighborhoods and is a perfect way for the newcomer to introduce yourself to the area or for the seasoned local to reacquaint yourself with some of the rich history of the area and the modernism of its desert architecture.

Head west on Ramon Road and turn right on Cahuilla Road. Watch the speed humps on this street. This neighborhood is called Tennis Club. The Community Church of Palm Springs is at the corner of Baristo Road and Cahuilla Road. It was built in 1935 and Dwight Eisenhower was said to have attended church here. Its Gothic revival elements are unique in Palm Springs.

Turn left on Tahquitz Canyon Way and then veer right on Museum Road and continue past the Palm Springs Desert Museum at 101 Museum Drive. This architecturally innovative building is striking and almost blends into the hillside. It is both an art museum and natural and local history museum.

Follow Museum Drive as it curves right then left past Desert Fashion Plaza and becomes Belardo Road. At Alejo Drive turn left and ride by the Old Las Palmas neighborhood on your right. Alejo turns into Vine Avenue, then Patencio Road. Turn left at Crescent Drive then right on Via Monte Vista then quickly left again on Crescent Drive.

At Rose Avenue, turn right and enjoy the beautiful lawns and palm trees of Vista Las Palmas as you pedal north. Also note the large rocks on the hillside to the west. These are dry falls most of the year but you might see water flowing down them after a recent rain. The road begins to climb and then you must turn right onto Stephens Road with its nice desert landscaped yards in the Little Tuscany area. Elvis Presley and Robert Young owned homes in Little Tuscany. Turn right on Vine Avenue then left on Camino Norte, which curves left onto Vereda Norte.

At North Palm Canyon Drive turn right then left on Tachevah Drive. Pass the Wellness Park on your right. As you head east you ride through Movie Colony, Ruth Hardy Park and then Sun Villas neighborhoods. Cross Sunrise Way and then turn right on Farrell Drive at the T intersection.

When you cross Alejo Road you ride into the Sunrise Park area. Past Ramon Road, Los Compadres neighborhood is on your left. After 2 miles turn right on Mesquite Avenue then left on Sunrise Way. The Deepwell area is on your right (see the Deepwell Tour ride). Stay right as it turns into La Verne Way as you enter Canyon North. Continue to South Palm Canyon Drive and turn right. Mesa/Cahuilla Hills is on your left. Turn left on Sunny Dunes Road then right onto Belardo Road and head back to your starting point at Ramon Road.

GETTING THERE

The ride can start anywhere on the loop but parking is readily available near the intersection of Ramon Road and Belardo Road. From South Palm Canyon Drive turn west on Ramon Road to Belardo Road and park here.

AMENITIES

Plenty of restaurants are available in this area for post ride nourishment.

Trip W4 - Deepwell Tour

Starting Point	East Palm Canyon Drive, Palm Springs
Distance	2.5 miles
Elevation Gain/Loss	50'/50'
Riding Time	30 minutes
Difficulty	Easy, not technical
Road Conditions	City streets
Season	Fall, Winter, Spring
Equipment	Any bicycle
Optional Topo Map	Palm Springs, CA

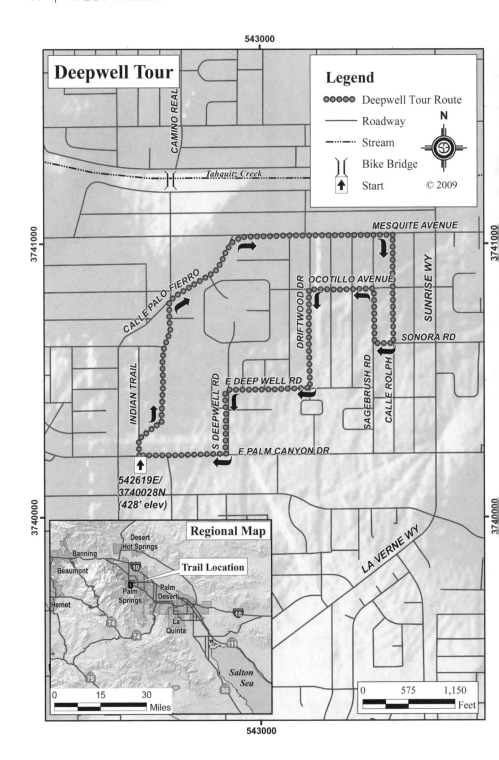

Deepwell Tour

543000

CAMINO REAL

Tahquitz Creek

Legend

⦿⦿⦿⦿⦿ Deepwell Tour Route

—— Roadway

--·--·-- Stream

⊐⊏ Bike Bridge

⬆ Start   © 2009

N

3741000

MESQUITE AVENUE

CALLE PALO FIERRO

DRIFTWOOD DR

OCOTILLO AVENUE

SUNRISE WY

SONORA RD

CALLE ROLPH

SAGEBRUSH RD

INDIAN TRAIL

S DEEPWELL RD

E DEEP WELL RD

E PALM CANYON DR

⬆

542619E/
3740028N
(428' elev)

3740000

Regional Map

Desert
Hot Springs

Banning

Beaumont

10

Palm
Springs

Palm
Desert

Hemet

74

La
Quinta

74

79

86

10

111

Salton
Sea

Trail Location

LA VERNE WY

0   15   30
Miles

0   575   1,150
Feet

543000

Deepwell is one of the most desirable neighborhoods in the Palm Springs area and has a very fascinating history. This area was initially occupied by the Agua Caliente Band of Cahuilla Indians and was later sold and owned by a number of people who initially farmed the area. In the mid 1920s water was hit with a 100' well. The well was extended to over 600', which gave the area its name. A guest ranch was later built and existed until the late 1940s. At that time the area was subdivided and many of the streets were named after the desert flora—Manzanita, Ocotillo, Mesquite, and Sagebrush to name a few.

In the 1950s and 1960s a number of celebrities as well as other local notables began settling in the neighborhood. This ride will pass by several of these residences and will definitely give you a flavor of this area with its nice homes and immaculate desert style gardens.

Begin riding north on Indian Trail and immediately angle right on Camino Real. Follow Camino Real to Calle Palo Fierro and follow it to the right. Turn right on Mesquite Avenue and then right on Calle Rolph. Carmen Miranda, the Latin dancer known for her hoop skirt and a basket of fruit on her turbaned head lived at 1044 Calle Rolph in the late 1940s. 1290 Calle Rolph was the home of the actress Marorie Main who achieved popularity as a comedienne in a number of 1940s movies but is best known as the character "Ma Kettle" for the remainder of her career.

Turn right at Sonora Road and right once more at Sagebrush Road. The home at 1349 was owned by the Jerry Lewis family. Turn left at Ocotillo Avenue and again left at Driftwood Drive. The famous actor William Holden resided at the large estate at 1323 in the mid 60s to 70s. Phil Moody a musician and owner of Moody's Supper Club lived at 1440 Driftwood.

Turn right at Deepwell Road. The ride will continue west but a short up and back on Manzanita will take you by Liberace's second desert home at 1516, Eva Gabor's house at 1350 and Loretta Young's house at 1075. To continue, follow Deepwell Road west, passing the Deepwell Ranch, and then south to East Palm Canyon Drive. Turn right at East Palm Canyon Drive passing the Biltmore and then turn right at Indian Trail to end the ride.

GETTING THERE

Take South Palm Canyon Drive to East Palm Canyon Drive and park on the side of the road just north on Indian Trail. Note that this ride does not follow the Deepwell bike route signs exactly. Follow these direction,s as we will be riding through some of the inner streets in Deepwell.

Trip W5 - Canyon Country Club Route

Starting Point	La Verne Way, South Palm Springs
Distance	5 miles
Elevation Gain/Loss	75'/75'
Riding Time	45 minutes
Difficulty	Easy, not technical
Road Conditions	City streets
Season	Fall, Winter, Spring
Equipment	Any bicycle
Optional Topo Map	Palm Springs, CA

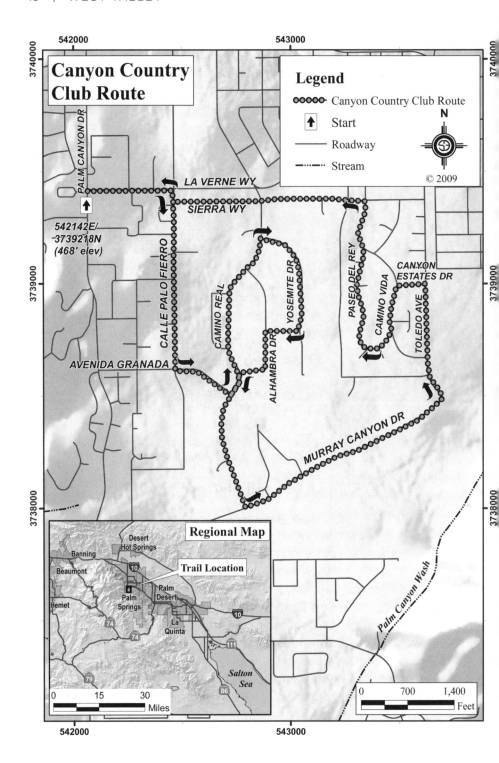

Canyon Country Club Route

Legend

○○○○○ Canyon Country Club Route

↑ Start

— Roadway

·····— Stream

© 2009

N

542142E/
-3739218N
(468' elev)

PALM CANYON DR

LA VERNE WY

SIERRA WY

CALLE PALO FIERRO

CAMINO REAL

YOSEMITE DR

ALHAMBRA DR

PASEO DEL REY

CAMINO VIDA

CANYON ESTATES DR

TOLEDO AVE

AVENIDA GRANADA

MURRAY CANYON DR

Regional Map

Desert Hot Springs

Banning

Beaumont

Trail Location

Hemet

Palm Springs

Palm Desert

La Quinta

74

74

79

10

10

111

86

Salton Sea

0   15   30
Miles

Palm Canyon Wash

0   700   1,400
Feet

In 1960 a complicated negotiation with the Agua Caliente Indian tribe secured the 550 acre site for the Canyon Country Club. Billy Bell, a famous golf course architect, designed two 18-hole championship golf courses. The north, Canyon Country Club, opened first and wound its way through the famous Canyon region with its mid-century homes and beautiful views. At that time it was difficult to get to the course since I-10 did not exist and Indian Avenue was gravel. Soon a deal was made with the nearby famous Racquet Club where members could join both. Many celebrities then began golfing and buying homes on the course.

In 1963 the south course opened to the public and the Canyon Inn Hotel at Murray Canyon and South Palm Canyon Drive opened as well. In 2006 the Canyon Country Club changed its name to Palm Springs National Golf & Country Club. This ride will take you through some of the streets around the beautiful golf course.

Head east on La Verne Way and turn right on Calle Palo Fierro and enter Canyon South II neighborhood. Turn left at Avenida Granada, a wide quiet street with the golf course on your left. Turn left again at Camino Real. Follow it to Yosemite Drive and turn right. Keep your eye out for a large fountain in the middle of the golf course in the distance behind the homes. Turn right at Sequoia Place and pass by the golf course on both sides and the fountain, if running, should be visible on your left. Turn left at Alhambra Drive.

Back at Camino Real turn left through this heavily landscaped street and then left at Murray Canyon Drive. Head east as you pass by Indian Canyons Golf Course on your right and Palm Springs National on your left. Veer left at South Toledo Avenue.

Turn left at Canyon Estates Drive and approach the country club. Turn left at Madrona Drive and follow it right onto Paseo Del Rey as it winds its way south and then north. Stay left as it changes to Madrona Drive. At Sierra Way turn left and cross the north end of the golf course on this beautiful route and turn right on Calle Palo Fierro then left on La Verne to return to your car.

GETTING THERE

Take South Palm Canyon Drive to La Verne Way and park on the street in this area. Note that this ride does not follow the Canyon Country Club Loop bike route signs. Follow these directions as we will be riding through some of the inner streets in the area.

AMENITIES

Plenty of restaurants are available north of this area for post ride nourishment.

Trip W6 - South
Palm Canyon Ride

Starting Point	South Palm Canyon Drive, Palm Springs
Distance	7 or 10 miles out and back
Elevation Gain/Loss	370'/370' 2% average, 4–5% near end of canyon
Riding Time	1–1.5 hours
Difficulty	Moderate, not technical
Road Conditions	City streets. Admission fee required
Season	Fall, Winter, Spring
Equipment	Any bicycle
Optional Topo Map	Palm Springs, CA

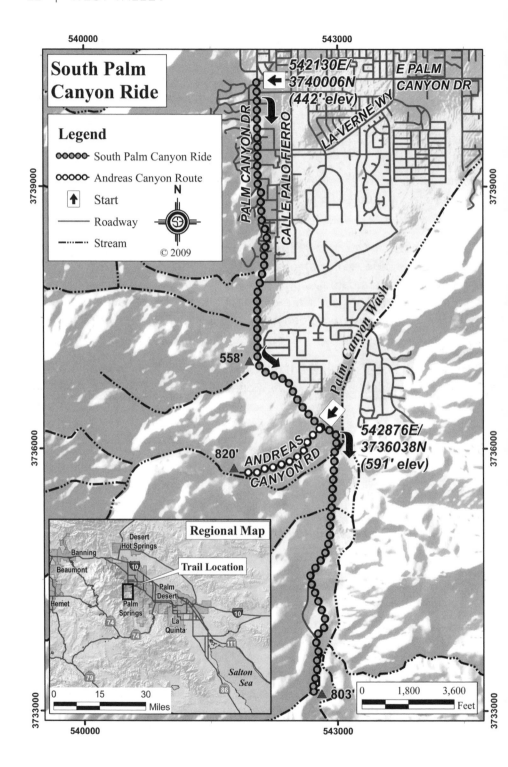

South Palm Canyon Ride

Legend

ooooo South Palm Canyon Ride

ooooo Andreas Canyon Route

⬆ Start

—— Roadway

-----⋅⋅⋅ Stream

N

© 2009

542130E/
3740006N
(442' elev)

E PALM
CANYON DR

PALM CANYON DR

CALLE PALO FIERRO

LA VERNE WY

Palm Canyon Wash

558'

542876E/
3736038N
(591' elev)

820'

ANDREAS
CANYON RD

803'

Regional Map

Desert
Hot Springs

Banning

Beaumont

Trail Location

Hemet

Palm
Springs

Palm
Desert

La
Quinta

Salton
Sea

0   15   30
Miles

0   1,800   3,600
Feet

Hundreds of years ago ancestors of the Agua Caliente Cahuilla Indians lived in the Palm Springs area. They frequented the many canyons here including Palm, Andreas, and Murray canyons. Water and food was readily available enabling them to grow crops and flourish. One of these canyons, Palm Canyon, is 15 miles long and is the world's largest California Fan Palm Oasis. The California Fan Palm, Washingtonia filifera, is the only native palm tree in the area and can be found in a number of natural oases in the area.

This ride starts just south of the busy streets in Palm Springs and slowly climbs its way into quiet Palm Canyon where you can enjoy the beauty of the canyon and see the California Fan Palms up close. Some bicyclists do this as a training ride and others as a quiet getaway from the city. You can ride to the end of Andreas Canyon for a total of 7 miles round-trip or to the end of Palm Canyon for 10 miles round-trip, or do both. Optional hikes can also be done along cool creeks where water flows year-round in case you get too warm bicycling the road.

Start riding south on South Palm Canyon Road and pass by the Mesa/Cahuilla Hills neighborhood on your right and Canyon North on your left. Once past Murray Canyon and Bogert Trail, Canyon South is on your left. Complicated negotiations with the Agua Caliente Band of Cahuilla Indians in 1960 secured 550 acres for the Canyon Country Club. The north opened first and then the south in 1963. In 2006 the Club changed its name to Palm Springs National Golf & Country Club.

As the road curves left you leave the golf courses and houses behind and start heading toward Palm Canyon. Pay your fee at the entrance station and start riding into the canyon. Andreas Canyon is on your right and it's less than a mile to the end of the road and the parking area. A nice hike on the north side of the creek where cool water flows year-round provides a wonderful place to relax or to stretch your legs a bit. Picnic tables are nearby. Near the parking lot, there is an area where Native American women once ground up berries and seeds into paste for food.

To do the longer ride, continue on Palm Canyon Road. It slowly rises as the hills begin to narrow. When you reach the first palm trees the road dips and passes by a unique rock formation. Watch for cars in this narrow section. The road then climbs steeply to the gravel parking area. The trading post is here as well as a picnic area nearby. If you have a way to secure your bike, you can hike among the palms below and imagine what life was like when the Indians lived here.

To finish the ride, head back down Palm Canyon Road returning the way you came.

GETTING THERE

Take South Palm Canyon Drive to the junction of East Palm Canyon Drive and park just south of East Palm Canyon Drive. The canyon is open 8 a.m. to 5 p.m. and in July through September only Friday through Sunday. There is an admission fee of $8 for adults. You can purchase a 6 month pass for $45 and yearly passes are also available. Many cyclists buy the 6 month pass late in the year and enjoy this ride many times before summer arrives. Bicycles are only allowed on the paved roads.

AMENITIES

A trading post with cold drinks and snacks is next to the parking lot at the end of the road. Restrooms are available, however there is no water for filling your bottles, so bring plenty along.

Trip W7 - Tahquitz Creek Tour

Starting Point	Demuth Park, Palm Springs
Distance	5 miles
Elevation Gain/Loss	75'/75'
Riding Time	45 minutes
Difficulty	Easy, not technical
Road Conditions	City streets
Season	Fall, Winter, Spring
Equipment	Any bicycle
Optional Topo Map	Palm Springs, CA

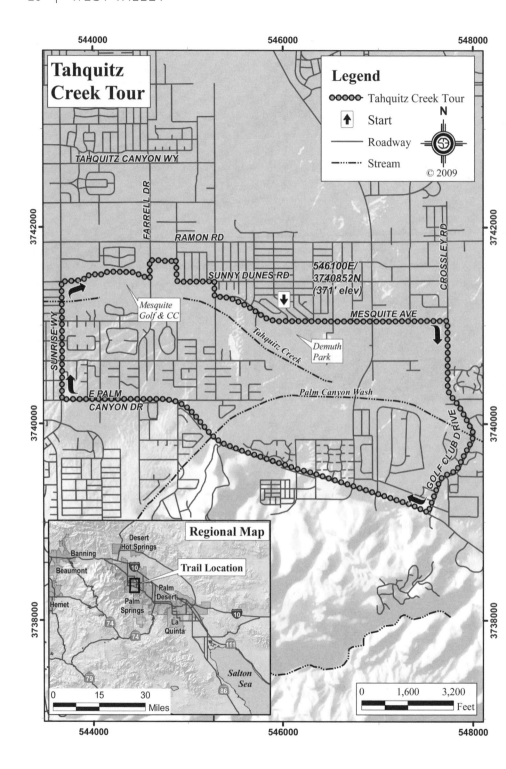

Tahquitz Creek Tour

Legend

- ○○○○○ Tahquitz Creek Tour
- ⬆ Start
- —— Roadway
- –·–·– Stream

© 2009

N

544000   546000   548000

3742000

3740000

3738000

TAHQUITZ CANYON WY

FARRELL DR

RAMON RD

SUNNY DUNES RD

546100E/
3740852N
(371' elev)

CROSSLEY RD

Mesquite
Golf & CC

MESQUITE AVE

Tahquitz Creek

Demuth
Park

SUNRISE WY

E PALM
CANYON DR

Palm Canyon Wash

GOLF CLUB DRIVE

Regional Map

Desert
Hot Springs

Banning

Beaumont

Trail Location

Palm
Desert

Hemet

Palm
Springs

La
Quinta

Salton
Sea

0   15   30
Miles

0   1,600   3,200
Feet

544000   546000   548000

Tahquitz Creek has its headwaters in the San Jacinto Wilderness and winds its way down through the Santa Rosa Mountains and the Agua Caliente Indian Reservation to Palm Springs. From there it joins Palm Canyon Wash and the Whitewater River to continue east past I-10. This ride follows part of the creek's path and travels the Tahquitz Creek Parkway alongside the Mesquite Country Club.

From Demuth Park head east on Mesquite Avenue. Cross Gene Autry Trail and turn right on Crossley Road. You pass by the Tahquitz Creek Golf Resort and soon the road changes its name to Golf Club Drive. Signs indicate you share the bike lane with golf carts. The Palms Oasis is on your left and Plaza Resort and Spa on your right. Once at East Palm Canyon Drive turn right and follow it 2.6 miles to Sunrise Way.

Turn right on Sunrise Way and at Desert Chapel Road turn right. A Desert Chapel Church and High School are located here. At the end of the road take the bike path across the wooden bridge and over Tahquitz Creek onto the north side of the Mesquite Golf and Country Club. The multiuse bike path goes for 0.5 miles along the beautiful golf course and several small ponds.

At Farrell Drive, go left on the sidewalk and look for a sign on the other side of the street indicating a continuance of the bike path. Cross Farrell when safe and follow the bike path east onto the golf course again. It quickly comes to Compadre Road where you turn right and you can stay on the sidewalk or on the road and follow as it curves left and becomes Sunny Dunes Road.

At Cielo Road go right and then left onto Mesquite Avenue and ride along the golf course and back to Demuth Park and your car.

GETTING THERE

From Gene Autry Trail turn west onto Mesquite Avenue. Demuth Park has a number of places you can park to start the ride.

AMENITIES

Demuth Park has bathrooms and water available.

Trip W8 - Goat Trails

Starting Point	South Palm Canyon Drive, Palm Springs
Distance	3–5 miles with various loop options
Elevation Gain/Loss	600'/100' (one way) 12% grade in places, varies on route
Riding Time	2–3+ hours depending on route
Difficulty	Moderate, some technical spots and a few steep spots
Road Conditions	Dirt road and trails
Season	Fall, Winter, Spring
Equipment	Mountain bike
Optional Topo Map	Cathedral City, CA

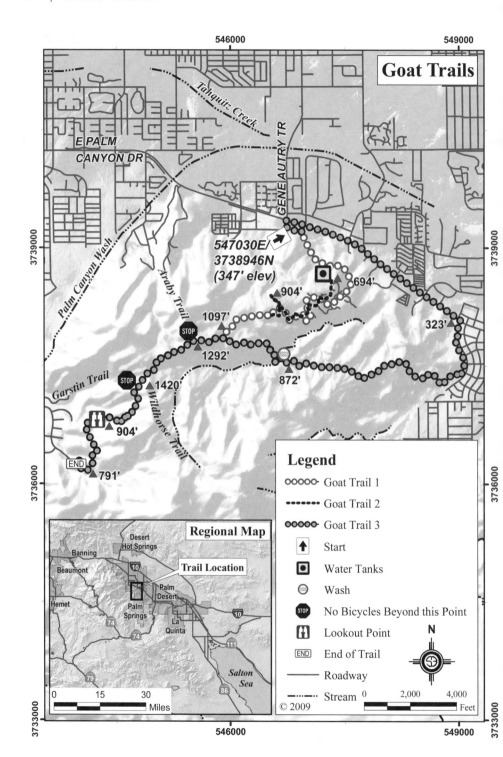

Goat Trails

547030E/
3738946N
(347' elev)

Legend

○○○○○ Goat Trail 1

•••••••• Goat Trail 2

◎◎◎◎◎ Goat Trail 3

⬆ Start

◉ Water Tanks

◉ Wash

🛑 No Bicycles Beyond this Point

🚻 Lookout Point

[END] End of Trail

— Roadway

••••••• Stream

Regional Map

Trail Location

© 2009

N

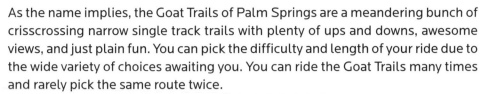

As the name implies, the Goat Trails of Palm Springs are a meandering bunch of crisscrossing narrow single track trails with plenty of ups and downs, awesome views, and just plain fun. You can pick the difficulty and length of your ride due to the wide variety of choices awaiting you. You can ride the Goat Trails many times and rarely pick the same route twice.

Start by riding up the dirt road behind the gate just to the south of the Rimrock Shopping Center and Vons. The road is an easy climb past the tanks on your right but then swings west and turns into a 12% grind for a little while. Thankfully it tops out for a bit so you can catch your breath and enjoy the wonderful views of the desert valley below and Murray Peak to the south. From here the recommended route is to keep climbing on the road as far as you can and then pick any one of the single track routes that fits your ability and start the fun descent. Pick your way from trail to trail and climb back up if you want to try others. You can do this all day long or as long as your food, water, and legs hold out.

One option from here is to continue on the road east, which eventually comes to the junction of the Garstin, Thielmann and Wild Horse Trails. The only two authorized biking trails from here are the Wild Horse Trail heading up the ridge to the south and the Thielman Trail straight ahead. The Thielman Trail is 1.5 miles down with some steep rocky sections and then about 7 paved miles back to your car. The Wild Horse Trail goes south for a number miles of miles and is not covered here.

The Garstin, Shannon, Berns, Araby, and Henderson Trails are not authorized for bikes under the new trails plan. Please abide by these rules so we can continue to bike on the approved trails.

The recommended way down is to return the way you came. As you head back, you may see a road junction that heads southeast up a small hill and drops into Eagle Canyon, which is another way out, albeit with some paved riding to get back to your car. Note that there are proposals to develop the property where Eagle Canyon Trail dumps out (west of the flood control channel), which might make this route questionable in the future. There are a few steep sections to watch out for this way, so unless you are feeling adventurous, your best bet is to return the way you came back to the Rimrock Shopping Center.

GETTING THERE

Take Highway 111 to the Rimrock Shopping Center at 4721 South Palm Canyon Drive. It intersects with Gene Autry Trail. Park in the parking lot south of Vons or on the nearby street. The ride starts on the unpaved road with the gate just south of the shopping center.

AMENITIES

Refreshments and restrooms are available in the nearby shopping center.

Trip W9 - Cathedral City Tour

Starting Point	Vista Chino and Landau, north Cathedral City
Distance	12 miles (plus optional side trips)
Elevation Gain/Loss	50'/200' one way
Riding Time	1 hour
Difficulty	Easy, not technical
Road Conditions	City streets
Season	Fall, Winter, Spring
Equipment	Any bicycle
Optional Topo Map	Cathedral City, CA

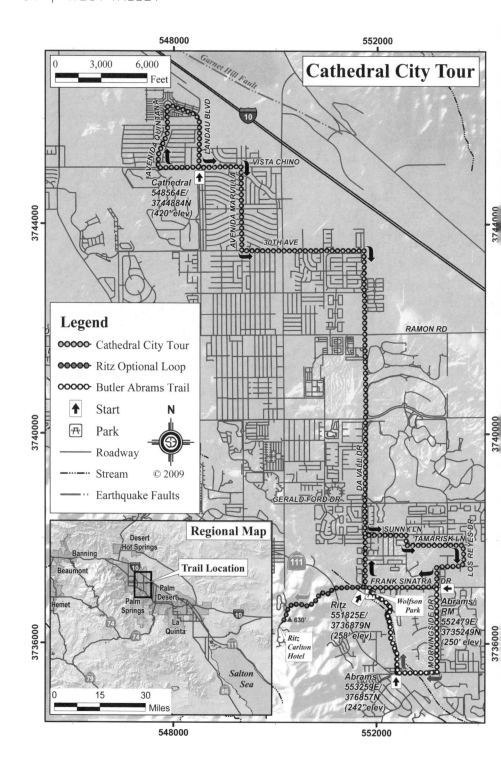

Cathedral City Tour

0   3,000   6,000
Feet

Garnet Hill Fault

VISTA CHINO

Cathedral
548564E/
3744884N
(420' elev)

30TH AVE

RAMON RD

Legend

ooooo⊶ Cathedral City Tour

ooooo⊶ Ritz Optional Loop

ooooo⊶ Butler Abrams Trail

↑ Start   N

🏕 Park

—— Roadway

---·--- Stream   © 2009

—--·· Earthquake Faults

GERALD FORD DR

DA VALL DR

SUNNY LN
TAMARISK LN

LOS REYES DR

Regional Map

Desert
Hot Springs

Banning

Beaumont

Trail Location

Palm
Desert

Hemet

Palm
Springs

La
Quinta

630'

Ritz
Carlton
Hotel

Salton
Sea

FRANK SINATRA DR

Ritz
551825E/
3736879N
(258' elev)

Wolfson
Park

Abrams/
RM
552479E/
3735249N
(250' elev)

MORNINGSIDE DR

Abrams
553259E/
376857N
(242' elev)

0   15   30
Miles

Cathedral City is situated between Palm Springs and Rancho Mirage and like most areas of the Coachella Valley was first inhabited by the Cahuilla Indians. In 1850 Colonel Henry Washington of the U.S. Army Corps of Engineers named the nearby canyon Cathedral Canyon because it reminded him of the interior of a large cathedral. In 1925 the first subdivision in the area was called Cathedral City and not until 1981 was the city incorporated and is now the third largest city in the area. It has a number of championship golf courses, luxurious country clubs and shopping areas.

This ride will start in the northern reaches of Cathedral City and head south giving you a flavor of the area riding past a number of exclusive golf courses and neighborhoods. From the starting point near Vista Chino and Landau Boulevard head west on Vista Chino. Turn right at Avenida Quintana and enter Rio Vista indicated by the stone marker. Stay straight through two roundabouts and at a large fenced desert-like playground veer right. You can do a quick circle around the loop if you want. Stay right onto Rio Vista Drive and pass by the wash on your left with native vegetation including mesquite and other desert plants and trees.

At Vista Chino turn left and then right onto Avenida Maravilla. At Tachevah Drive you pass by Panorama Park on your right with water and restrooms. Turn left at 30th Avenue, a nice wide street with bike lanes. Ride 1.5 miles and turn right on Da Vall Drive. You pass Century Park and then once past Ramon Road the Mission Hills - Gary Player Golf Course is on your left. Cross Dinah Shore Drive and the Mission Hills Country Club is on your left.

Once past Gerald Ford Drive turn left on Sunny Lane and enter the quiet well kept neighborhoods surrounding the Tamarisk Country Club just south of here. This is technically Rancho Mirage, but I'm sure you won't mind the small detour into this beautiful area. Turn right on Palm View Road then left on Tamarisk Lane. After this wonderful stretch of road turn right on Los Reyes Drive. Curve right onto La Paz Road past Iris Lane and stay left as it turns into Thompson Road.

Turn right on Frank Sinatra Drive. One of the options below starts at this spot. Continue west and just before Da Vall Drive the Michael S. Wolfson Park is on your left. This is a great opportunity to refill your water bottle, have a snack and look at the beautiful vegetation and the Santa Rosa Mountains to the south.

After your break, head north on Da Vall Drive and follow it 7.7 miles past the Mission Hills Country Club back to 30th Avenue. Turn left on 30th and follow it to Avenida Maravilla and left on Vista Chino to return. At 30th you can also continue to Landau Boulevard and turn right to return to the start at Vista Chino.

OPTIONS

Ritz Carlton Climb - 2.4 miles roundtrip 10% grade

This is a thigh-burner climb and only for those who like climbing. Instead of turning right on Da Vall Drive, stay straight on Frank Sinatra Drive. Drop into the Whitewater Wash dip and then cross Highway 111. The Rancho Mirage City Hall is on your left and the beautiful Ritz Carlton waterfall on your right. The climb starts immediately then flattens out briefly and then climbs sharply again. Climb to the gated entrance or turn around when you've had enough. Head back on Frank Sinatra Drive to Da Vall Drive and turn left to continue the ride. Note that just south of the Rancho Mirage City Hall is a wonderful Cancer Survivor's Park with water, shade and messages about cancer if you want to rest after the climb.

Butler Abrams Side Trip - 2.6 miles

Instead of turning right on Frank Sinatra Drive, stay straight on Thompson Road, which turns into Morningside Drive past Frank Sinatra Drive. You pass by Waterford and the Springs Country Club on the left and Morningside Club on the right. The signs on this scenic divided road indicate that you should share the bike lane with golf carts. Turn right on Country Club Drive and pass by another entrance to Morningside. The road dips as you cross over the golf course and just before Highway 111 look for a block wall on your right and a small bike path sign just past that labeled Butler - Abrams Trail. Curve back on the sidewalk here and follow that path north alongside the Morningside Golf Course. Soon you dip quickly into the wash and up the other side. Sometimes the trail can be sandy in the bottom and of course avoid it during wet times. Follow the trail to the Michael S. Wolfson Park where you can refill your water bottle and enjoy the view of the Santa Rosa Mountains to the south. From here head north on Da Vall Road to continue the ride.

If the wash bottom is impassable, instead of turning right on the bike path continue straight on Country Club Drive and just before Highway 111 ride onto the sidewalk and turn right. This is a shared bike and pedestrian sidewalk but you can also choose to ride on the road. Ride 1.3 miles and turn right on Frank Sinatra Drive and dip into the Whitewater River channel crossing and back to Michael S. Wolfson Park and Da Vall Road to continue.

GETTING THERE

From I-10 take the Date Palm exit and head south. Turn right on Vista Chino and park near the intersection of Vista Chino and Landau Boulevard. If you want to start near the southern end of the ride, you could park by Michael S. Wolfson Park at the corner of Frank Sinatra Drive and Da Vall Drive and follow the Butler Abrams Trail southeast from the park and reverse the route described above.

AMENITIES

Water is available at Michael S. Wolfson Park and Panorama Park on Avenida Maravilla at Tachevah Drive.

Trip C1 - Rancho Mirage Scenic Tour

Starting Point	Michael S. Wolfson Park, Rancho Mirage
Distance	7 miles
Elevation Gain/Loss	100'/100'
Riding Time	45 minutes
Difficulty	Easy, not technical
Road Conditions	City streets
Season	Fall, Winter, Spring
Equipment	Any bicycle
Optional Topo Map	Cathedral City, CA

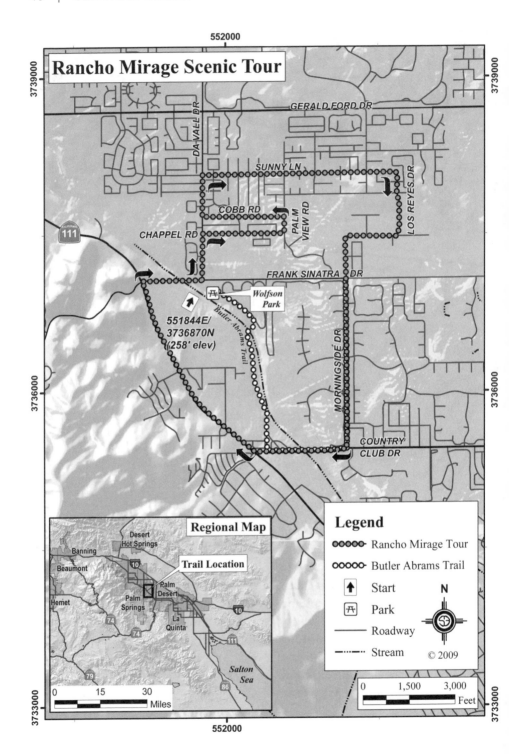

Rancho Mirage Scenic Tour

552000

3739000

GERALD FORD DR

DA VALL DR

SUNNY LN

LOS REYES DR

COBB RD

PALM VIEW RD

CHAPPEL RD

111

FRANK SINATRA DR

Wolfson Park

551844E/
3736870N
(258' elev)

Butler Abrams Trail

MORNINGSIDE DR

3736000

COUNTRY CLUB DR

Regional Map

Trail Location

Desert Hot Springs

Banning

Beaumont

10

Palm Desert

Hemet

Palm Springs

74

La Quinta

74

111

79

Salton Sea

86

0   15   30
Miles

Legend

○○○○○ Rancho Mirage Tour

○○○○○ Butler Abrams Trail

↑ Start

🏕 Park

— Roadway

---- Stream

N

© 2009

0   1,500   3,000
Feet

3733000

Rancho Mirage is nestled between Cathedral City to the west and Palm Desert to the east and hugs the base of the picturesque Santa Rosa Mountains to the south. Rancho Mirage was incorporated in 1973 by merging Mirage Cove with five unincorporated areas described as the "Cove communities" of Desert, Magnesia, Palmas, Tamarisk, and Thunderbird. It now hosts 12 golf courses/country clubs, and a number of celebrities and political figures have vacationed here over the years. On the quieter side, Rancho Mirage is careful to balance all of this with a number of parks and trails for enjoyment of the desert habitat and scenery.

This ride starts at one of those beautiful small parks and provides an optional section on one of the multiuse urban trails with great views of the mountains and the nearby Morningside Country Club. Michael S. Wolfson Park is 1.7 acres and has a water fountain and a drinking fountain and a number of native plants and benches from where you can enjoy the view of the Santa Rosa Mountains.

Begin the ride by heading north on Da Vall Drive past Tamarisk West. Turn right on Chappel Road and enjoy the beautiful palm tree-lined street and nice yards of this neighborhood that surrounds the Tamarisk Country Club. Turn left on Palm View Road and then left on Cobb Road, with views of San Jacinto Mountain in the distance.

Turn right on Da Vall Drive and then right again on Sunny Lane and pass by the gated communities of Casas de Seville and Viento. After this nice stretch of road curve right on Los Reyes Drive and note the exclusive gated community Artisan on your left. Signs here indicate you should share the road with golf carts.

Curve right onto La Paz Road past Iris Lane and stay left as it turns into Thompson Road. Cross Frank Sinatra Drive and stay straight as the name changes to Morningside Drive. You pass by Waterford and the Springs Country Club on the left and Morningside Club on the right. Again, signs on this scenic divided road indicate that you should also share the bike lane with golf carts.

Turn right on Country Club Drive and pass by another entrance to Morningside. The road dips as you cross over the golf course and just before Highway 111 look for a block wall on your right and a small bike path sign just past the sign labeled Butler - Abrams Trail. Curve back on the sidewalk here and follow that path north alongside the Morningside Golf Course. Soon you dip quickly into the wash and up the other side. Sometimes the trail can be sandy in the bottom and of course avoid it during wet times (see Options). Follow the trail back to the Michael S. Wolfson Park.

OPTIONS

If the Whitewater River crossing on the Butler Abrams Trail is wet or too sandy for your bicycle, instead of turning right on the bike path continue straight on Country Club Drive and just before Highway 111 ride onto the sidewalk and turn right. This is a shared bike and pedestrian sidewalk but you can also choose to ride on the road. Ride 1.3 miles and turn right on Frank Sinatra Drive and dip into the Whitewater River channel crossing and back to the starting point at the Michael S. Wolfson Park.

GETTING THERE

Take Highway 111 to Frank Sinatra Drive. Pass over the Whitewater Wash dip and park by Michael S. Wolfson Park near the corner of Da Vall Drive.

AMENITIES

Water is available at the park.

A number of restaurants are available for a post-ride feed on Highway 111/Palm Canyon Drive.

Trip C2 - Bump and Grind Trail

Starting Point	Painters Path Road, Rancho Mirage
Distance	4.5 miles out and back (plus optional side trip)
Elevation Gain/Loss	1300'/320' – 11% average grade with a few steeper sections
Riding Time	2 hours
Difficulty	Difficult, some technical spots
Road Conditions	Dirt road
Season	Fall, Winter, Spring
Equipment	Mountain bike
Optional Topo Map	Rancho Mirage, CA

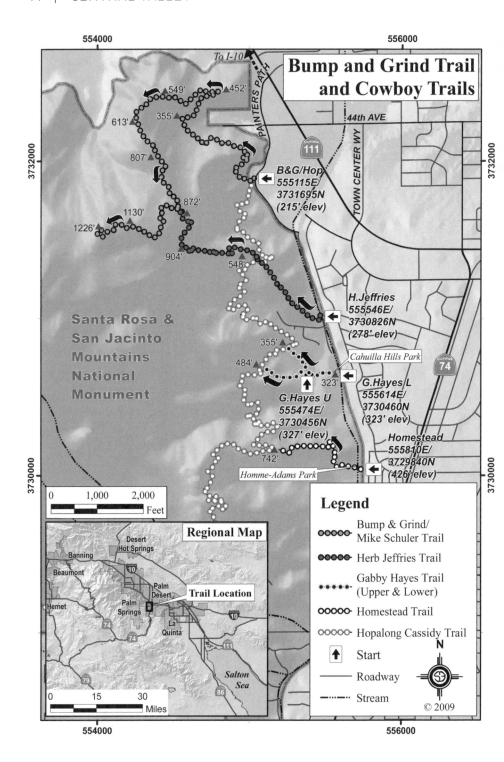

Bump and Grind Trail and Cowboy Trails

554000

556000

To I-10

549'

452'

PAINTERS PATH

44th AVE

613'

355'

111

807'

TOWN CENTER WY

B&G/Hop
555115E/
3731695N
(215' elev)

1130'

872'

1226'

904'

548'

H.Jeffries
555546E/
3730826N
(278' elev)

Santa Rosa &
San Jacinto
Mountains
National
Monument

355'

484'

Cahuilla Hills Park

74

323'

G.Hayes L
555614E/
3730460N
(323' elev)

G.Hayes U
555474E/
3730456N
(327' elev)

Homestead
555810E/
3729840N
(426' elev)

742'

Homme-Adams Park

3732000

3732000

3730000

3730000

0   1,000   2,000
Feet

Legend

Regional Map

Desert
Hot Springs

Banning

Beaumont

10

Palm
Desert

Trail Location

Hemet

Palm
Springs

74

La
Quinta

10

111

74

79

Salton
Sea

86

0   15   30
Miles

Bump & Grind/
Mike Schuler Trail

Herb Jeffries Trail

Gabby Hayes Trail
(Upper & Lower)

Homestead Trail

Hopalong Cassidy Trail

Start

Roadway

Stream

N

© 2009

554000

556000

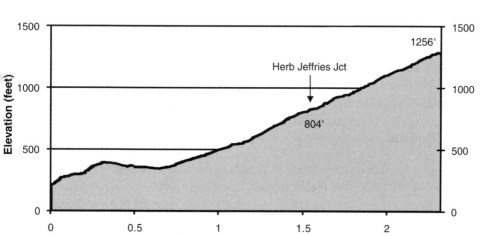

The Bump and Grind Trail, also known as the Desert Mirage Trail (and Dog Poop Trail for the ubiquitous dogs on the trail), is easily one of the most popular trails in the Valley. There are great views of Rancho Mirage, Palm Desert, Coachella Valley, and the towering Santa Rosa Mountains behind.

This ride starts at an elevation of 250 feet and climbs to almost 1300 feet in just over 2.25 miles making it a rather strenuous climb. There are always lots of hikers, people walking dogs, and joggers to make the climb more interesting as you maneuver your way up the trail. With an 11% average grade and some short sections even steeper, it will be a difficult or strenuous effort depending on your fitness level.

The views of the surrounding area are wonderful and you will undoubtedly have time to check them out when you stop to catch your breath now and then. The new trailhead at Painters Path was rerouted in 2008 from the Magnesia Falls neighborhoods. Traffic and private property made that a controversial starting area. Please respect the local's wishes and use the new trailhead that also provides access to the wonderful Hopalong Cassidy Trail area (see The Hopalong Cassidy Trail ride).

Two trails start from the Painters Path Trailhead. The Hopalong Cassidy Trail heads south, while the Bump and Grind heads west and then north. The first 0.6 miles of the trail to the junction of the main road is actually called the Mike Schuler Trail. Mike created most of the trails in this area. The trail starts climbing and soon you are above the shopping center with a nice view of the surrounding area. Quickly you encounter some sharp switchbacks that may require you to walk a bit. At the crest the trail swoops down and across a nice canyon above a nursery and then climbs to join the main wide dirt road to the peak.

Right from this junction takes you down to Desert Drive and the old trailheads whose use are not authorized. Stay left and start the main climb. At about 1 mile a narrow trail joins from the right coming up from the old trailhead and soon another one joining from a small ridge on the right as well. These are very narrow and not suitable for both hikers and bicyclists. After another 0.5 miles you have three route choices. I recommend taking the right path around a small hill, which is more gentle and provides nice views to the west and northwest.

At about 1.75 miles, when the trail curves right, the Herb Jeffries Trail intersects from the left. This is an alternate way back to the starting point but has some fairly steep and narrow switchbacks to negotiate and not recommended for all riders. See Options.

Once you near the top it feels like it gets steeper, but the last mile or so is a fairly constant 12% grade. Avoid the narrow, short, steep climb to your left as you near the top and stay right around the base of the final hilltop. It is a tad longer but is an easier final climb. The section you just passed is better left for the way down.

Congratulations, you made it! The view is well worth the work. Watch your speed on the way down and yield to hikers and other riders on the trail.

OPTIONS

On the way down an alternate route back to the Painters Path Trailhead is to take the Herb Jeffries Trail. It intersects from the right, about 0.5 miles from the top, when the road makes a sweeping left curve. It has some fairly steep narrow switchbacks and is definitely more technical, but you will encounter less people. You will meet the Hopalong Cassidy Trail on your right. Stay straight and a short distance further the trail curves left around a small knob and then quickly heads down the final 0.9 mile to the Painters Path Trailhead.

GETTING THERE

From Highway 111 take Fred Waring Boulevard west and turn left at the T intersection onto Painters Path Road. Follow that behind the shopping center just past a fenced area on your right and park there. The trail starts at the base of the hill on your right. A sign used to mark the trailhead but only the base is left.

AMENITIES

Restaurants are available in the surrounding shopping areas.

Trip C3 - Cahuilla Hills "Cowboy" Trails

Starting Point	Palm Desert
Distance	1.5 to 3.5 miles
Elevation Gain/Loss	Varies, maximum of 1000'/1000'– 4–12% average grade
Riding Time	1–1.5 hours depending on route
Difficulty	Moderate, some slightly technical spots
Road Conditions	Dirt trails
Season	Fall, Winter, Spring
Equipment	Mountain bike
Optional Topo Map	Rancho Mirage, CA

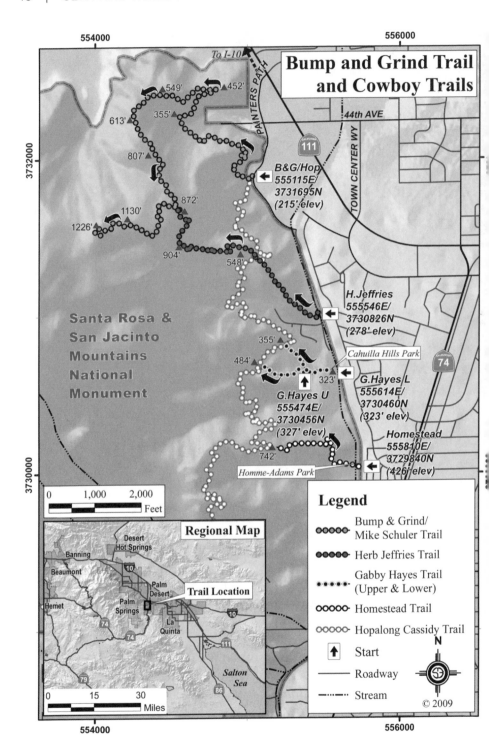

554000

556000

Bump and Grind Trail and Cowboy Trails

To I-10

PAINTERS PATH

44th AVE

TOWN CENTER WY

549'   452'

613'   355'

807'

872'

1130'

1226'

904'

548'

B&G/Hop
555115E/
3731695N
(215' elev)

Santa Rosa &
San Jacinto
Mountains
National
Monument

355'

484'

323'

H.Jeffries
555546E/
3730826N
(278' elev)

Cahuilla Hills Park

G.Hayes L
555614E/
3730460N
(323' elev)

G.Hayes U
555474E/
3730456N
(327' elev)

Homestead
555810E/
3729840N
(426' elev)

742'

Homme-Adams Park

74

0   1,000   2,000
Feet

Legend

Regional Map

Desert
Hot Springs

Banning

Beaumont

Palm
Desert

Palm
Springs

La
Quinta

Hemet

Trail Location

Salton
Sea

0   15   30
Miles

Bump & Grind/
Mike Schuler Trail

Herb Jeffries Trail

Gabby Hayes Trail
(Upper & Lower)

Homestead Trail

Hopalong Cassidy Trail

Start

Roadway

Stream

N

© 2009

3732000

3730000

554000

556000

Palm Desert is famous for its resorts, golf courses, and spas but what sets it apart is the variety of multiuse trails created to provide access to the nearby Santa Rosa and San Jacinto Mountains National Monument. This ride describes several "link" trails that provide easier access to the Hopalong Cassidy Trail. But these trails are short and fun to join together into rides of varying lengths depending on how much time you have.

The Herb Jeffries Trail is a tribute to Herb Jeffries, the legendary "Bronze Buckaroo," a recording artist and film star. He was popular in western movies and was a former Palm Desert resident who spoke at the trail dedication on April 2, 2005.

The Gabby Hayes Trail is named for George "Gabby" Hayes who performed a variety of roles in movies. He was well known for playing a grizzled codger who used phrases like "yer durn tootin" and "consarn it." He played Windy Halliday, the sidekick to Hopalong Cassidy, in a number of movies.

The Hopalong Cassidy Trail is named after William Boyd, a movie and popular cowboy hero who lived in the Palm Desert area. His cowboy screen name, Hopalong Cassidy, came from a broken leg he sustained shooting the first movie when he said "Oh, I'll manage to hop along." The trail was dedicated on January 31, 2004.

It is probably easiest to start at the Cahuilla Hills Park Trailhead. From here you can take the Gabby Hayes link then head south on Hopalong Cassidy and then down the Homestead Trail and back along the drainage channel to your start for about 650' elevation gain and 1.7 miles. Or turn right on Hopalong and ride 0.9 miles to Herb Jeffries and down 0.4 miles to the bottom or continue north on Hopalong for 0.9 miles to the Painters Path Trailhead. From there head south on Painters Path Road and at the end of the shopping center behind Target turn right, before the drainage channel, and pedal back to your car.

If you want to start at the Cap Homme-Ralph Adams Park Trailhead, the Homestead Trail link is a short 0.5 mile connector to the Hopalong Cassidy Trail but gains 340' for about 12.8% average grade. This trail was named for the homestead parcels in the area in the late 1800s and early 1900s. Start by climbing the short steep road that flattens out at a palapa shade cover with a water fountain and great views of the surrounding area. The concrete pad for the palapa was once part of the foundation of a homestead house. The trail continues climbing and meets the Hopalong Cassidy Trail partway up the ridge. Stay right and quickly drop down to the Gabby Hayes Trail in 0.9 mile. Follow the drainage channel road right to return to your car.

Starting at the Painters Path Trailhead, head south on the Hopalong Cassidy Trail. In 0.9 miles and 325' of elevation gain you reach the Herb Jeffries Trail. You can head left and down and then left again at the bottom to return. Or continue on Hopalong 0.9 miles to the Gabby Hayes Trail and down or continue another 0.9 miles to the Homestead Trail and down.

GETTING THERE

There are several places you can start this ride. There is parking at the Cap Homme-Ralph Adams Park, a 27-acre park, which provides access to the Homestead Trail link, Cahuilla Hills Park, a 27.5 acre park where the Gabby Hayes Trail link starts, or to extend the hike further at the Painters Path Trailhead of the Hopalong Cassidy and Mike Schuler Trails. The easiest place to start is Cahuilla Hills Park.

To reach the Cahuilla Hills Park Trailhead from Highway 111 turn south on Highway 74 and in 0.4 mile turn right on Pitahaya Street. Proceed to Edgehill Drive and turn left. Follow Edgehill as it curves right onto Tierra de Oro and cross the bridge. Parking is available by the tennis courts. The trail starts near the Gabby Hayes Trail marker next to the tennis courts and heads up the small canyon to the west to the right of the houses.

For the Cap Homme-Ralph Adams Park Trailhead from Highway 111 turn south on Highway 74 and after 1 mile turn right and then left on Thrush Road before the Palm Desert Community Church. Head across the small bridge and turn right when you see the Cap Homme-Ralph Adams Park stone marker. The parking area is a short distance on your left. The Homestead Trail starts at the base of the hill to the west and climbs toward the palapa shade cover.

For the Painters Path Trailhead, from Highway 111 take Fred Waring Boulevard west and turn left at the T intersection onto Painters Path Road. Follow that behind the shopping center just past a fenced area on your right and park there. The trail starts at the base of the hill on your right. A sign used to mark the trailhead but only the base is left. Take the Hopalong Cassidy Trail heading south. This adds 0.9 mi to the ride.

AMENITIES

Restaurants are available in shopping areas near the Painters Path Trailhead. Water is available at the base of the Homestead Trail and at the palapa shade cover partway up the trail.

Trip C4 - Hopalong Cassidy Trail

Starting Point	Painters Path Road or Art Smith Trailhead, Palm Desert
Distance	10 miles one way (plus options to shorten the ride)
Elevation Gain/Loss	3060'/3170' – 6–9% average grade with a few steeper sections
Riding Time	3 hours
Difficulty	Strenuous, technical, steep and narrow in places
Road Conditions	Dirt trail
Season	Fall, Winter, Spring
Equipment	Mountain bike
Optional Topo Map	Rancho Mirage, CA

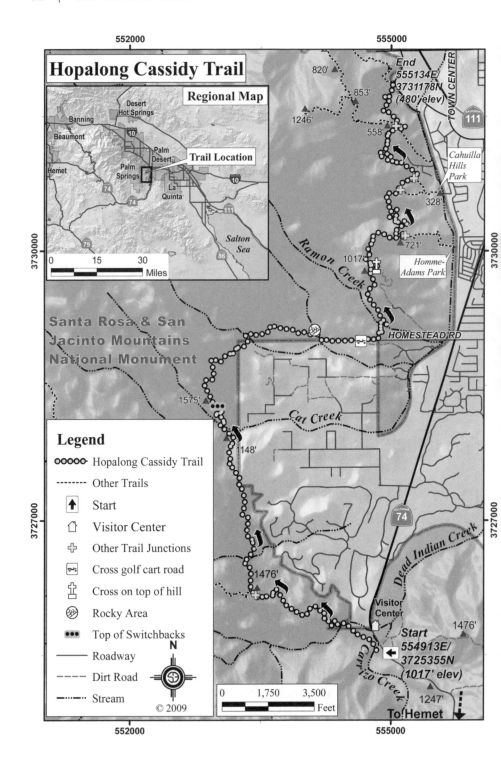

Hopalong Cassidy Trail

Regional Map

Trail Location

Desert Hot Springs

Banning

Beaumont

Hemet

Palm Desert

Palm Springs

La Quinta

Salton Sea

0   15   30
Miles

Santa Rosa & San Jacinto Mountains National Monument

End
555134E/
3731178N
(480' elev)

820'
853'
1246'
558'
1017'
721'
328'

Cahuilla Hills Park

Homme-Adams Park

HOMESTEAD RD

TOWN CENTER

Ramon Creek

Cat Creek

1575'
1148'
1476'

Dead Indian Creek

Visitor Center

Start
554913E/
3725355N
(1017' elev)

Carrizo Creek

1476'
1247'

To Hemet

Legend

○○○○○ Hopalong Cassidy Trail

------- Other Trails

↑ Start

⌂ Visitor Center

✚ Other Trail Junctions

Cross golf cart road

Cross on top of hill

Rocky Area

••• Top of Switchbacks

—— Roadway

---- Dirt Road

—••—• Stream

© 2009

N

0   1,750   3,500
Feet

552000
555000
3730000
3727000

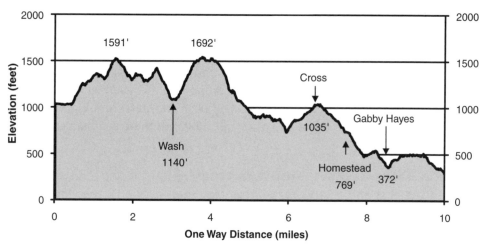

The Hopalong Cassidy Trail, ridden in its entirety, is nothing short of amazing. It climbs, it drops, it switchbacks and seems to hang in midair, contouring along hillsides with great views of golf courses and expensive houses below. This is almost as technical as the Art Smith Trail and the last or first 2.5 miles, depending on where you start the ride, is on the Art Smith Trail. If you're up for a little adventure and great views, this is a fun, challenging ride.

The trail is named after William Boyd, a movie and popular cowboy hero who lived in the Palm Desert area. His cowboy screen name, Hopalong Cassidy, came from a broken leg he sustained shooting the first movie when he said "Oh, I'll manage to hop along." The trail was dedicated on January 31, 2004.

There are several places this ride can be started. The Painters Path or Art Smith Trailheads are the most common if you want to ride the whole length. This description starts at the Art Smith Trailhead, which starts at a higher elevation and generally trends downhill. See Options for other ride choices.

From the Art Smith Trailhead parking area start riding north along the base of the levee to your right. The trail then swings left, crosses a small open area and you then start the moderately steep climb up a south facing slope. Soon the trail levels out a bit and heads north. Turn right when you see a Canyon Trail sign on your left. That ridge route trail is not approved for use. The trail will swing west past a tank below on your right. Brittle bush, barrel cactus flowers, and many other flowers color the landscape in the spring.

Look to the right to see the Hopalong Cassidy Trail contouring its way north on the hillside in the distance where you will be riding in a few minutes. Continue a short distance until you see the Hopalong Cassidy Trail sign at about 1.4 miles. Turn right and begin your journey. The trail trends downhill in this section with some nice ups and downs. Soon the trail drops into a canyon with occasional lavender bushes in the wash. Cross the sandy wash and start climbing a series of fairly sharp switchbacks where you may walk a bit, but there is a nice view from the top as a reward.

For the next half mile or so the narrow trail hugs the hillside and has some great views to the east and northeast. You can also look back and see Highway 74 and the Art Smith Trailhead parking area. Keep your eye out for the many barrel cacti dotting the hillside.

Soon the trail parallels a chain link fence that drops you quickly down to the edge of a golf course grassy area. Carefully follow the small rocky slope down and continue on the trail. It continues to parallel the fence and soon a dirt road on your right as well. Stay next to the fence on the trail and when it ends, go left across the paved golf cart road and continue the trail directly on the other side.

Soon you descend some steep switchbacks into a narrow high walled canyon. Bulrushes, red chuparosa, brittle bush, and desert lavender grow alongside a small trickle of water. After leaving the small canyon you should see the cross ahead of you on top of a large hill. A nice climb takes you to the top of the hill with great views all around. Relax, you've earned it.

Stay straight past the cross (don't take the left here, which heads toward the fence and a paved golf cart road on the other side) and start a nice descent around the head of a small canyon. The trail then drops rather steeply down a ridge and you soon meet the Cap Homme-Ralph Adams Park Trail that continues straight down the ridge for 0.5 miles. This is the first bailout if you want to cut the ride short with a 2.5 mile paved climb back to your car. There is water at the shade palapa 0.5 miles below. To continue, go left at the junction.

From here the trail descends quickly and passes on your right two junctions for the Gabby Hayes Trail that starts in the Cahuilla Hills Park area. Again, you can take either of these side routes down to end the ride here and have about 3 paved miles back to your car. To continue, stay heading generally north and keep to the left at the next few junctions you encounter.

In 0.75 mile the trail meets the Herb Jeffries Trail, which intersects from the left. Stay right here and you quickly pass on your right the other side of the Herb Jeffries Trail, which drops down rather steeply to the wash below. Stay left at this second junction and follow the trail as it curves left around a small knob and then heads down the final 0.9 mile to the Painters Path Trailhead. Congratulations, you have completed this memorable ride. It is about 5 miles on the pavement back to the Art Smith Trailhead.

OPTIONS

There are several places you can start and end this ride to shorten the distance or to do the ride in sections over several trips. The traditional starting points are the two ends of the trail at the Art Smith or the Painters Path Trailheads. The total one way distance in either direction is 10 miles not including riding on pavement to get back to your car (about 5 miles). You can also start or end at Cap Homme-Ralph Adams Park, Cahuilla Hills Park, or the Herb Jeffries Trail just north of Cahuilla Hills Park making loops of various lengths. The Cahuilla Hills "Cowboy" Trails ride provides descriptions of these shorter loops and where to park.

GETTING THERE

Since this is a one-way ride, you have your choice of where to start this ride, at the Painters Path Trailhead or the Art Smith Trailhead. The Art Smith Trailhead is generally more downhill since you start 800 feet higher than Painters Path, but with all the undulations on the trail the actual difference is only a couple hundred feet. You have to decide if you want to ride up or down Highway 74 for about 5 miles to return to your car after the ride unless you do a car shuttle. To start from the Art Smith Trailhead, from Highway 111 take Highway 74 for 4 miles to the Art Smith Trailhead on your right just past the entrance to the Santa Rosa and San Jacinto Mountains National Monument visitor center.

For the Painters Path Trailhead, from Highway 111 take Fred Waring Boulevard west and turn left at the T intersection onto Painters Path Road. Follow that behind the shopping center just past a fenced area on your right and park there. The trail starts at the base of the hill on your right. A sign used to mark the trailhead but only the base is left. Make sure you take the trail heading south. North is the Mike Schuler Trail.

AMENITIES

Restaurants are available in shopping areas near the Painters Path Trailhead. Water is available at the shade palapa 0.5 miles below Hopalong on the Homestead Trail and at the Santa Rosa and San Jacinto Mountains National Monument visitor center.

Trip C5 - Living Desert Hill Climb

Starting Point	Civic Center Park, Palm Desert
Distance	19 miles
Elevation Gain/Loss	900'/900'
Riding Time	1.5 – 2 hours
Difficulty	Moderate, not technical, hill climb
Road Conditions	City streets
Season	Fall, Winter, Spring
Equipment	Any bicycle
Optional Topo Maps	Rancho Mirage, La Quinta, CA

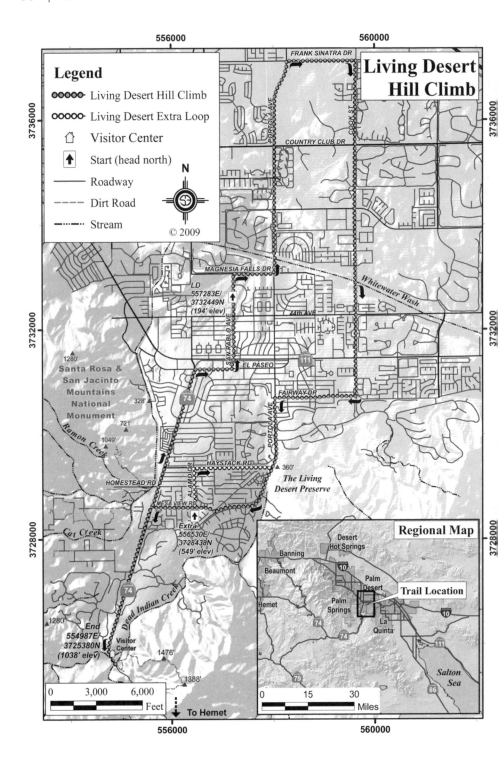

Living Desert Hill Climb

Legend

- ⦿⦿⦿⦿ Living Desert Hill Climb
- ⦾⦾⦾⦾ Living Desert Extra Loop
- ⌂ Visitor Center
- ⬆ Start (head north)
- —— Roadway
- ---- Dirt Road
- -··-··- Stream

© 2009

N

FRANK SINATRA DR

COUNTRY CLUB DR

PORTOLA AVE

HWY 111

MAGNESIA FALLS DR

Whitewater Wash

LD
557283E/
3732449N
(194' elev)

44th AVE

EL PASEO

111

SAN PABLO AVE

1280'
Santa Rosa &
San Jacinto
Mountains
National
Monument

328'

721'

1049'

Ramon Creek

74

FAIRWAY DR

PORTOLA AVE

HAYSTACK RD

360'

The Living
Desert Preserve

ALAMO DR

HOMESTEAD RD

MESA VIEW RD

Cat Creek

Extra
556530E/
3728438N
(549' elev)

74

Dead Indian Creek

1280'

End
554987E/
3725380N
(1038' elev)

Visitor
Center

1476'

1388'

Regional Map

Desert
Hot Springs

Banning

Beaumont

10

Palm
Desert

Trail Location

Hemet

Palm
Springs

74

74

La
Quinta

10

111

79

Salton
Sea

86

0   3,000   6,000
Feet

0   15   30
Miles

To Hemet

This ride takes you past one of the most unique places in the Coachella Valley, the Living Desert. It is described as a zoo and endangered species conservation center, botanical garden, natural history museum, wilderness park, nature preserve, and education center. The Palm Springs Desert Museum established a nature center and interpretative trail in 1970 on 360 acres here. It has grown to over 1200 acres today. This ride starts in the populated areas of Palm Desert and works its way past the Living Desert and then heads up Highway 74 to the Santa Rosa and San Jacinto Mountains National Monument visitor center. Imagine what the area would be like without these permanent wilderness preserves providing places for people to learn about and enjoy the natural habitat.

From Civic Center Park head north on San Pablo Avenue. Turn right on Magnesia Falls Drive then left on Portola Avenue. Continue north about 2.5 miles past several beautiful country clubs including Chaparral, Santa Rosa, and Desert Willow to Frank Sinatra Boulevard. Turn right on Frank Sinatra Boulevard and then right on Cook Street. Follow Cook Street south for 4 miles past the other side of the same country clubs. Cross Highway 111 and turn right on Fairway Drive. At Portola Avenue turn left and just before Buckboard Road you will pass by the Living Desert on your left.

Portola will curve right past Ironwood Country Club and at Mesa View you must turn right and begin the gentle climb up this beautiful palm-lined, divided street to Highway 74. Watch for golf carts sharing the lane. Some riders wanting more of a workout do several loops here by turning right at Alamo Drive, right at Haystack Road, right on Portola Avenue to complete the circuit. To continue, carefully cross Highway 74 and ride about 2 miles up to the visitor center entrance on your left. Water and restrooms as well as information and books about the surrounding area are available at the visitor center bookstore. The newly published Santa Rosa & San Jacinto Mountains National Monument map is available here.

Reverse your route and head back down Highway 74. Turn right at El Paseo just before Highway 111. Watch for window shopping drivers on this street. Turn left on San Pablo Avenue and cross Highway 111 back to your starting point.

GETTING THERE

From Highway 111 head north on San Pablo Avenue. Park in the area around Civic Center Park.

AMENITIES

Water and restrooms are available at the Santa Rosa and San Jacinto Mountains National Monument visitor center. Several bagel and coffee shops frequented by bicyclists after riding this loop are nearby just west of Highway 74 on El Paseo and off of Town Center Way north of Highway 111.

Trip C6 - Coachella Valley Preserve and Dillon Road Ride

Starting Point	Civic Center Park, Palm Desert
Distance	48 miles
Elevation Gain/Loss	1550'/1550'
Riding Time	4 hours
Difficulty	Moderate to Difficult, not technical
Road Conditions	City streets
Season	Fall, Winter, Spring
Equipment	Any bicycle
Optional Topo Maps	Rancho Mirage, Cathedral City, Myoma, West Berdoo Canyon, Indio, La Quinta, CA

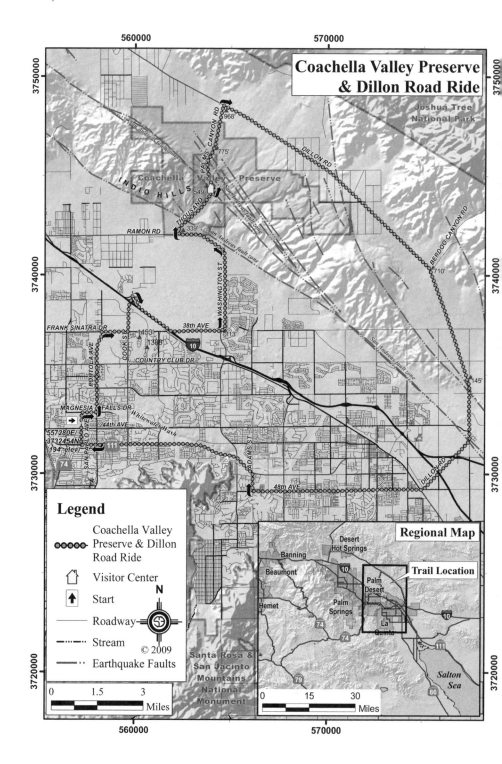

This ride follows the route of one of the Desert Bicycle Club Saturday morning rides. The Desert Bicycle Club is a recreational cycling club whose objective is to promote cycling activities in the Coachella Valley. The club promotes bicycling as a lifetime activity that encourages good health, wellness, friendship, and personal accomplishment. This is one of their premier rides that could be described as a grand tour of Palm Desert, the Coachella Valley Preserve area, Indio, La Quinta, and Indian Wells.

Head north on San Pablo Avenue then right on Magnesia Falls Drive. Turn left on Portola Avenue and ride for 2.5 miles past several picturesque country clubs to Frank Sinatra Drive. Turn right and ride past the Santa Rosa Country Club and the Desert Willow Golf Resort and turn left on Cook Street. Follow Cook over I-10 and turn right on Varner Avenue and parallel the freeway for a short distance. At 38th Avenue turn left, then left again at Washington Street.

North of Avenue 38, and once past the Mountain Vista Golf Club, you pass through a few miles of the Coachella Valley Preserve, designed to protect the Coachella Valley fringe-toed lizard. The lizard is an indicator of rich life on desert sand dunes and as development encroaches, 20,000 acres of the viable dune habitat are preserved here as well as 20 miles of hiking trails.

The road begins to gently climb as you head north on Washington Street. The road will curve left and at Thousand Palms Road turn right. Soon you head into Thousand Palms Canyon as the alluvial hills begin to narrow. The road bends left around Squaw Hill and in a short distance the entrance to the Coachella Valley Preserve visitor center and Paul Wilhelm Grove is on your left. Springs along the Mission Canyon Fault and Banning Fault, parallel lines of the San Andreas Fault System running through this area, provide the necessary water for the palms. The road continues climbing past another palm tree grove on the left and the canyon begins to open up as you head toward Dillon Road.

Turn right on Dillon Road and pedal for about 15 miles through rolling ups and downs as you pass by the Little San Bernardino Mountains on your left and the wildly contorted Indio Hills on your right. When you near the large power lines, Berdoo Canyon heads northeast but look to the west and note the almost vertical section of Indio Hills. This is a result of the action along the San Andreas Fault Zone where opposite sides of the fault slide past one another a couple of inches each year.

You will ride over the Coachella Canal and pass by the Vineyard Resort and Golf Course and soon cross under I-10 and then the 86S Expressway. Across Indio Boulevard the road changes names to Avenue 48. Follow Avenue 48 past several country clubs for 5.5 miles to Adams Street and turn right. Turn left on Highway 111 and follow it 5.8 miles to San Pablo Avenue and turn right to return to the start.

GETTING THERE

The ride begins in the parking lot of Palm Desert Civic Center Park next to the skate board park on Fred Waring just north of San Pablo.

AMENITIES

Several bagel and coffee shops frequented by bicyclists after riding this loop are nearby just west of Highway 74 on El Paseo and off of Town Center Way north of Highway 111.

Trip C7 - Palm Desert and La Quinta Loop

Starting Point	Civic Center Park, Palm Desert
Distance	40, 33, or 20 miles depending on route taken
Elevation Gain/Loss	760'/760' (40 mile loop)
Riding Time	2–3 1/2 hours depending on route
Difficulty	Moderate, not technical
Road Conditions	City streets
Season	Fall, Winter, Spring
Equipment	Any bicycle
Optional Topo Maps	Rancho Mirage, Cathedral City, Myoma, La Quinta, CA

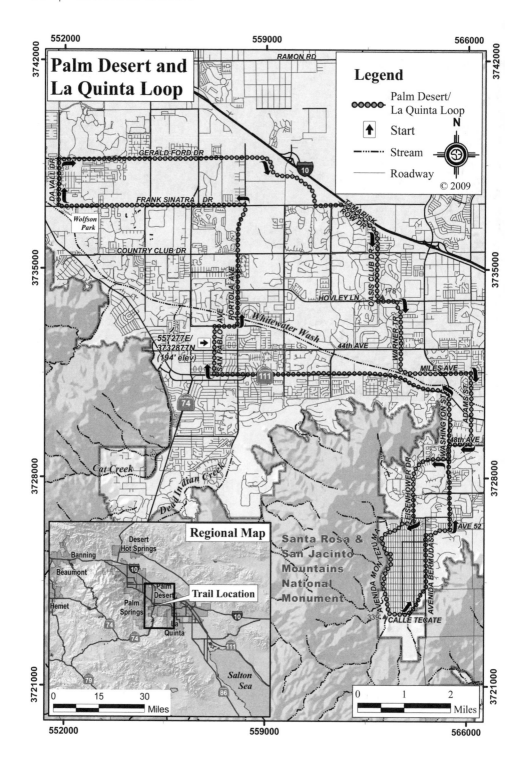

Palm Desert and La Quinta Loop

Legend

- ○○○○○ Palm Desert/La Quinta Loop
- ↑ Start
- ·····-·-·· Stream
- —— Roadway

N

© 2009

Regional Map

Trail Location

Santa Rosa & San Jacinto Mountains National Monument

This ride follows the route of one of the Desert Bicycle Club Saturday morning rides with a few options for shorter rides. The Desert Bicycle Club is a recreational cycling club whose objective is to promote cycling activities in the Coachella Valley. The club promotes bicycling as a lifetime activity that encourages good health, wellness, friendship, and personal accomplishment. This is a medium ride with several options that takes you through the cities of Palm Desert, Rancho Mirage, La Quinta, and Indian Wells.

Head north on San Pablo Avenue then right on Magnesia Falls Drive. Turn left on Portola Avenue and ride for 2.5 miles past several beautiful country clubs to Frank Sinatra Drive. You have a choice here. You can continue north to Gerald Ford Drive and then turn right, which cuts 7 miles from the ride or you can turn left and take Frank Sinatra Drive to Da Vall Drive, turn right there and then right on Gerald Ford Drive past the Mission Hills Country Club and back to this point.

Continue east on Gerald Ford Drive past the Marriot Shadow Ridge Resort and follow it as it makes several curves and intersects Frank Sinatra Drive. Turn left and then angle right onto Tamarisk Row, which parallels the railroad tracks and I-10 along a row of tamarisk trees. When you cross Country Club Drive the road changes to Oasis Club Drive.

Turn left on 42nd Avenue then right on Warner Trail. After Fred Waring Drive turn left on Miles Avenue and follow it past the Indian Wells Tennis Garden venue to Adams Street where you turn right. Cross the Whitewater River and then Highway 111 and turn right on Avenue 48 and pedal past Rancho La Quinta to Washington Street.

You have another option here. Turn right to cut 13.5 miles from the ride, or turn left on Washington and then right on Eisenhower Drive to head into the La Quinta Cove area. Follow it past La Quinta Resort and Club and turn right on Avenida Montezuma. Soon you begin a easy climb past many colorful southwest-style homes with a view of the nearby Santa Rosa Mountains. The Fred Wolff Bear Creek Trail bike path is to your right along this route and every now and then a small ramada with a bench and water fountain await if you want to fill your bottle. Take a brief left on Calle Ensenada then the second right on Avenida Juarez, which turns into Avenida Montezuma.

Once at the "Top of the Cove" stay left onto Calle Tecate. You will pass by two Cove Oasis Trailheads on your right that provide access to a 114-acre natural open space area with hiking and mountain biking trails. See the Cove Oasis Trails ride. Curve left onto Avenida Bermudas and enjoy the nice downhill run to Avenue 52.

Turn right there and then left on Washington Street and follow that 4 miles to Highway 111. Turn left on Highway 111 and follow it 5.8 miles to San Pablo Avenue and turn right to return to the start.

GETTING THERE

The ride begins in the parking lot of Palm Desert Civic Center Park next to the skate board park on Fred Waring just north of San Pablo.

AMENITIES

Several bagel and coffee shops frequented by bicyclists after riding this loop are nearby just west of Highway 74 on El Paseo and off of Town Center Way north of Highway 111.

Trip C8 - Randall Henderson Trail

Starting Point	Visitor center, Highway 74, Palm Desert
Distance	5 miles
Elevation Gain/Loss	400'/400' – 5.5 % average grade uphill
Riding Time	1.5 hours
Difficulty	Moderate, slightly technical in spots
Road Conditions	Dirt trail
Season	Late spring, summer, early fall
Equipment	Mountain bike
Optional Topo Map	Rancho Mirage, CA

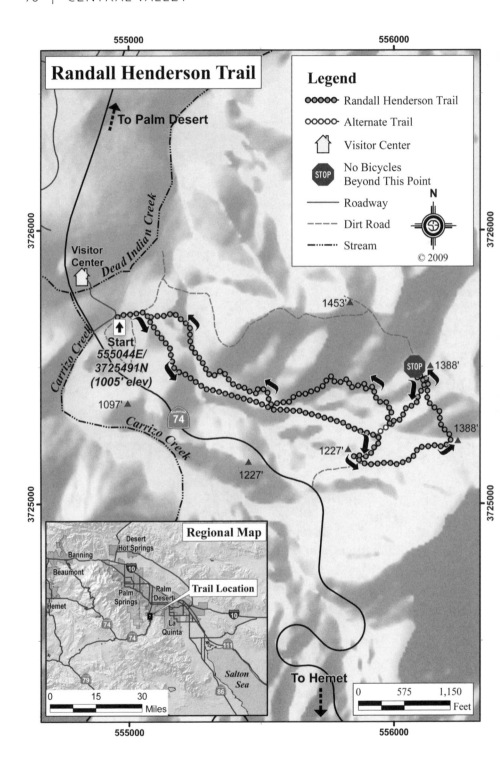

Randall Henderson Trail

Legend

⊙⊙⊙⊙⊙ Randall Henderson Trail

○○○○○ Alternate Trail

⌂ Visitor Center

🛑 No Bicycles Beyond This Point

—— Roadway

- - - - Dirt Road

·—··—·· Stream

© 2009

To Palm Desert

Dead Indian Creek

Visitor Center

Carrizo Creek

Start
555044E/
3725491N
(1005' elev)

1453'

STOP ▲ 1388'

1097' ▲

74

Carrizo Creek

1227' ▲

1227' ▲

1388' ▲

Regional Map

Desert Hot Springs

Banning

Beaumont

10

Palm Springs

Palm Desert

Trail Location

Hemet

74

74

La Quinta

10

111

Salton Sea

79

86

To Hemet

0   15   30
Miles

0   575   1,150
Feet

Randall Henderson was an author and an explorer of the desert. He was also involved in the early development of Palm Desert and documented its history and evolution in *Desert Magazine*, which he published in the 1930s through the 1960s. He was also founder of the Desert Protective Council, which promotes and protects the southwest deserts. The Randall Henderson Trail was dedicated in February of 2005 by members of his family.

The Randall Henderson Trail is a moderate loop through the diverse desert vegetation in this area and will provide a glimpse into the region he worked so hard to protect. You will ride by cacti, brittlebush, and many other desert plants. The trailhead monument is just inside the visitor center entrance on your right as the driveway curves left.

Once on the trail, at the first junction go right and soon you will begin climbing a small ridge with a dry wash on either side. In a short distance the trail drops into the wash on the right. Stay right and start an easy climb through a cholla field to a trail junction. Turn right and begin the slightly steeper climb over a small hill to a dirt road. A spur road on your right goes to a gate on Highway 74. Stay straight and follow the road as it curves uphill to the north. Nice views of the valley below and the Santa Rosa Mountains to the west and south highlight this stretch of road.

At the road closed gate, turn left and head down the nice single track. The closed road straight ahead is not authorized for travel. In the spring this area is highlighted with colorful yellow brittlebush flowers and views of snow-covered San Jacinto and San Gorgonio Mountains to the northwest. Soon a trail connects from the right. Take this trail, which begins a nice descent across the hillside below you and to the right of a small wash. When you meet the wash below you have two choices. You can stay left across the wash and then right to connect with the trail you rode from the visitor center and return that way. Another option is to follow the wash straight ahead. You will encounter some loose sandy sections and a small rocky section you have to walk your bike down. This wash route will eventually climb onto a small hill and then drop quickly down and rejoin the original trail at the first junction you encountered and head straight back to the starting point.

GETTING THERE

From Highway 111 take Highway 74 about 4 miles to the Santa Rosa and San Jacinto Mountains National Monument visitor center on your left. Park in the visitor center parking lot. The ride starts at the Randall Henderson trail marker just inside the entrance to the visitor center where the driveway curves north.

AMENITIES

Water and restrooms as well as information, maps, and books for the area can be found at the Santa Rosa and San Jacinto Mountains National Monument visitor center. The newly published Santa Rosa & San Jacinto Mountains National Monument map is available here.

Trip C9 - Art Smith Trail

Starting Point	Art Smith Trailhead, Highway 74, Palm Desert
Distance	16 miles out and back
Elevation Gain/Loss	2670'/1310' (one way) 7%–9% grade in places
Riding Time	5–6 hours
Difficulty	Strenuous, some technical spots
Road Conditions	Dirt trail, rocky in spots, some sand
Season	Fall, Winter, Spring
Equipment	Mountain bike, plenty of inner tubes, food, water
Optional Topo Map	Rancho Mirage, CA

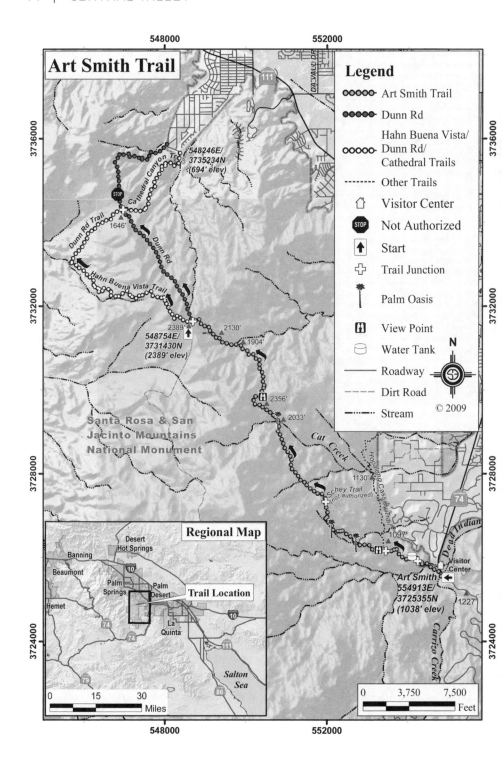

Art Smith Trail

548000   552000

Legend

- ●●●●● Art Smith Trail
- ●●●●● Dunn Rd
- ●●●●● Hahn Buena Vista/ Dunn Rd/ Cathedral Trails
- ------- Other Trails
- ⌂ Visitor Center
- 🛑 Not Authorized
- ⬆ Start
- ✚ Trail Junction
- 🌴 Palm Oasis
- 🔲 View Point
- ◎ Water Tank
- —— Roadway
- ----- Dirt Road
- ······· Stream

© 2009

N

548246E/
3735234N
(694' elev)

STOP

Cathedral Canyon Tr

Dunn Rd Trail

1646'

Dunn Rd

Hahn Buena Vista Trail

2389'
548754E/
3731430N
(2389' elev)

2130'

1904'

2356'

2033'

Santa Rosa & San
Jacinto Mountains
National Monument

Cat Creek

1130'

Schey Trail
(not authorized)

Honalua Casible Trail

74

1097'

Dead Indian

Visitor
Center

Art Smith
554913E/
3725355N
(1038' elev)

1227'

Carrizo Creek

Regional Map

Desert
Hot Springs

Banning

Beaumont

Palm
Springs

Palm
Desert

Trail Location

Hemet

10

La
Quinta

111

74

79

Salton
Sea

86

0   15   30
Miles

0   3,750   7,500
Feet

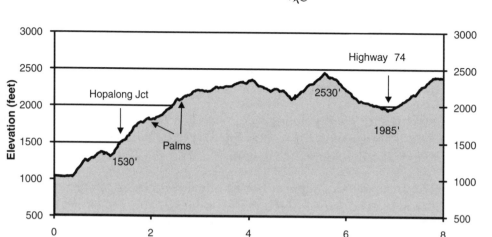

This is one of the most difficult rides in the book but also one of the most rewarding for those who are in good shape and like a technical challenge. The trail takes you into the beautiful Santa Rosa Mountains, where you will leave civilization behind and climb through hidden valleys and alongside several palm groves. You must be in great shape and carry plenty of water and snacks for this ride. It's best to ride with a few friends and make sure you have the equipment you need to repair flats and minor mechanical challenges. You might encounter cholla in the path at times so it's best to carry several tubes and a patch kit or use a slime-type product in your tubes.

With the newly established Coachella Valley Multiple Species Habitat Conservation Plan, the Art Smith Trail section above the intersection of the Hopalong Cassidy Trail to Dunn Road requires a self-issue permit. This is not fully defined yet and may be available at a kiosk at the trailhead or online with no limit on the number of permits available. It is part of a research program to determine the effects of non-motorized trail-based recreation on Peninsular bighorn sheep. Also note that this section of trail is closed from June 15 to September 30 for the bighorn sheep. The lower section up to and including the Hopalong Cassidy Trail does not require a permit and is open year-round. Please follow these new rules so we can all continue enjoying the trails.

From the Art Smith Trailhead parking area start riding north along the base of the levee to your right. The trail then swings left, crosses a small open area and you then start the moderately steep climb up a south facing slope. Soon the trail levels out a bit and heads north. Turn right when you see a Canyon Trail sign on your left. That ridge route trail is not approved for use. The trail will swing west past a tank below on your right. Brittle bush, barrel cactus flowers, and many other flowers color the landscape in the spring.

Look to the right to see the Hopalong Cassidy Trail contouring its way north on the hillside in the distance. At 1.4 miles you will pass the Hopalong Cassidy Trail on your right. This ride continues straight.

Soon the trail seems to disappear behind some low hills separating you from civilization below and you ride through an area full of barrel cactus and beautiful flowers. The trail turns rocky for the next mile or so and all but the best riders will most likely push their bikes through some of it.

Around 2 miles the trail drops into a couple of washes and the first palm grove. I counted 18 palm trees. Just past the palms the trail climbs steeply out of the wash and soon you pass by several more palm groves in the wash to your left. The trail levels out somewhat and you can enjoy some gentle ups and downs. At 3.2 miles you will pass the Schey Trail on the right. This trail is also not authorized for use, so we continue straight.

The trail climbs to a high spot where you have great views of the valley and mountains to the west and Haystack Mountain to the southwest. Around 5 miles the trail drops into a wash with palm trees and more farther up the wash. During springtime this area is very green.

The trail begins a nice downhill run and drops into a wash around the 7 mile mark. Follow the sign and angle left (southwest) and continue up the soft sand. Depending on the time of year, you may be able to ride part of the wash. In less than half a mile the trail climbs out of the wash and pretty quickly you reach Dunn Road. A tractor with a wooden sign: Mike Dunn Desert Riders Oasis and some picnic tables thankfully mark the end of the trail for a total of 8 miles. The Art Smith Trail 1977 sign is also here marking the top of the trail.

Nice views of San Jacinto and San Gorgonio Mountains to the north and Haystack Mountain to the south reward you for your effort. For this ride, the recommended return route is back down the Art Smith Trail the way you came. Left on Dunn Road is a long 12 mile, 2400' climb to Highway 74 and the Pinyon Flat area. An unmarked right turn (make the wrong turn and you will head into private ranches), three locked gates and private property signs should convince you not to head that way.

You can turn right on Dunn Road and ride 2 miles to the junction of the Dunn Road Trail coming from the left and the Cathedral Canyon Trail heading right. This junction is at the bottom of a hill with an open valley to your left before you start a slow climb north on Dunn Road. If you go this way you must take the Cathedral Canyon Trail right here and out through Cathedral City Cove below. There are some steep sections on this 1.5 mile trail and you will also have about a 13-mile ride on pavement back to your car. Continuing north on Dunn Road from this junction is not authorized and crosses posted private land.

The Hahn Buena Vista Trail intersects Dunn Road across from the Art Smith Trail here heading west over the hill in front of you. It connects with the Vandeventer Trail from which you can connect to the Wild Horse Trail to the Goat Trails. It is about 7 miles to that junction where you can go left 1.3 miles down the Thielman Trail and 20 paved miles to your car or right about 3 miles on the Goat Trails to the Rimrock Shopping Center and then about 13 miles on pavement back to your car. You would need to have plenty of daylight, energy, water, and snacks to take either route back. Note that the Garstin, Shannon, Berns, Araby, and Henderson Trails are not authorized for bicycles in that area.

It's important to note that continuing down the Vandeventer or Fern Canyon Trails into Palm Canyon is not allowed. They lead onto tribal lands in the Indian Canyons where bicycles are prohibited.

GETTING THERE

From Highway 111 take Highway 74 about 4 miles to the Art Smith Trailhead on your right just past the entrance to the Santa Rosa and San Jacinto Mountains National Monument visitor center.

AMENITIES

Water and restrooms as well as information, maps, and books for the area can be found at the Santa Rosa and San Jacinto Mountains National Monument visitor center to the left just before the turnoff for the Art Smith Trail. The newly published Santa Rosa & San Jacinto Mountains National Monument map is available here. It's best not to park in the visitor center lot in case you get back after the gate is closed.

Trip E1 - Bear Creek Trail

Starting Point	Fritz Burns Community Park, La Quinta
Distance	5.5 miles
Elevation Gain/Loss	350'/350'
Riding Time	45 minutes
Difficulty	Easy, not technical
Road Conditions	Bike path, city streets
Season	Fall, Winter, Spring
Equipment	Any bicycle
Optional Topo Map	La Quinta, CA

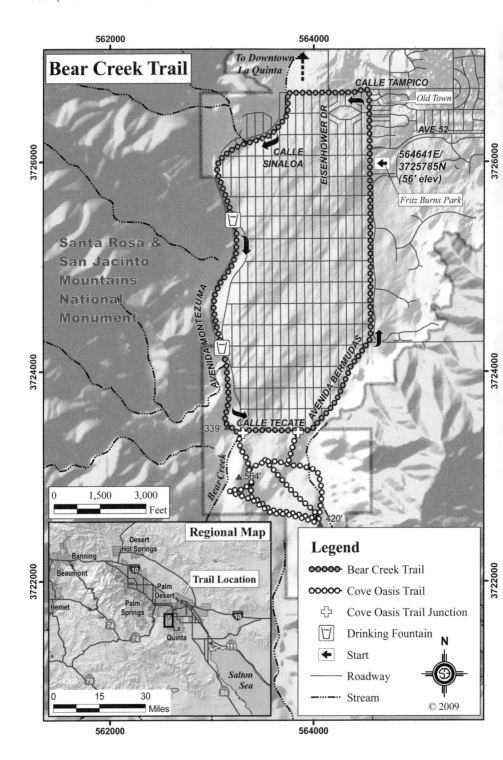

Bear Creek Trail

562000

564000

To Downtown La Quinta

CALLE TAMPICO

Old Town

EISENHOWER DR

AVE 52

CALLE SINALOA

564641E/ 3725785N (56' elev)

Fritz Burns Park

3726000

Santa Rosa & San Jacinto Mountains National Monument

AVENIDA MONTEZUMA

AVENIDA BERMUDAS

3724000

339'

CALLE TECATE

564'

Bear Creek

0   1,500   3,000
Feet

420'

Regional Map

Desert Hot Springs

Banning

Beaumont

10

Palm Desert

Trail Location

Hemet

Palm Springs

10

74

La Quinta

74

111

3722000

Salton Sea

79

86

0   15   30
Miles

Legend

●●●●● Bear Creek Trail

○○○○○ Cove Oasis Trail

✛ Cove Oasis Trail Junction

⊌ Drinking Fountain

◄ Start

— Roadway

▬▪▬▪▬ Stream

N

© 2009

562000

564000

The City of La Quinta is home to over 20 golf courses including the famous PGA West. They host the La Quinta Art Festival and have a splendid Old Town Village with shopping and dining. But when you want to get away from the activity and take in views of the desert beauty and surrounding Santa Rosa Mountains this easy ride is for you.

In 2003 the City of La Quinta purchased 19 acres of open space to preserve the natural desert land for future generations. The preserve is dedicated to Fred Wolff, La Quinta's first mayor who helped preserve public access to the nearby Santa Rosa Mountains. There are nature trails you can hike if you have the time, but this ride will concentrate on a multiuse path that skirts the edge of "The Cove" and hugs the nearby Santa Rosa Mountains. On the ride you will also see a variety of native plants including Blue Palo Verde, desert willow (pink flowers, small tree), brittlebush (yellow, daisy-like flowers), and fragrant desert lavender (purple flowers) to name a few.

From Fritz Burns Community Park, start pedaling north on Avenida Bermudas. Soon you will pass by the streets of La Quinta's delightful Old Town Village on your right. There are several opportunities for food and meandering here after the ride.

At Calle Tampico turn left, cross Eisenhower Drive and continue west on a nice bike path through palm trees. The bike path leads you to Avenida Carranza. Turn left and the Bear Creek Path is immediately on your right. The path parallels Avenida Montezuma for a short distance and passes many beautiful, colorful southwest style homes. As the bike path leisurely climbs, Eisenhower Peak is on your right and behind you Indio Mountain will be on your right. There are several ramadas with benches and water fountains on the path if you want to stop and enjoy the natural desert beauty and fill your water bottle.

Once you reach the top, the path will curve left, pass another ramada and take you onto Calle Tecate, which is the Top of the Cove. You will pass by two Cove Oasis Trailheads on your right that provide access to a 114 acre natural open space area with hiking and mountain biking trails. See the Cove Oasis Trails ride. Curve left onto Avenida Bermudas and enjoy the less than 2 mile nice downhill run back to your starting point.

GETTING THERE

From Highway 111 take Washington Boulevard south. Turn right on Avenue 52 then left on Avenida Bermudas. Park anywhere in or near Fritz Burns Community Park.

AMENITIES

Old Town La Quinta, just north of the starting point, is a great place to visit and get something to eat after the ride. You won't find big name establishments here but the charm of locally owned and operated shops. Water is available at several places on the bike path as well as at Fritz Burns Community Park.

Trip E2 - La Quinta Loop

Starting Point	Fritz Burns Community Park, La Quinta
Distance	24 miles (plus optional side trips)
Elevation Gain/Loss	400'/400'
Riding Time	2 hours
Difficulty	Moderate, not technical
Road Conditions	City streets
Season	Fall, Winter, Spring
Equipment	Any bicycle
Optional Topo Map	La Quinta, CA

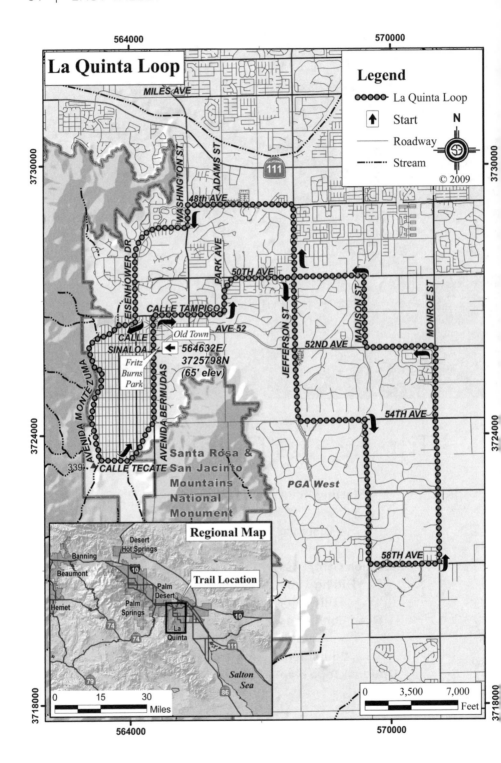

La Quinta Loop

Legend

⊙⊙⊙⊙ La Quinta Loop

↑ Start

Roadway

Stream

© 2009

N

564632E/
3725798N
(65' elev)

Old Town

Fritz
Burns
Park

Santa Rosa &
San Jacinto
Mountains
National
Monument

PGA West

Regional Map

Desert
Hot Springs

Banning

Beaumont

Palm
Desert

Trail Location

Hemet

Palm
Springs

La
Quinta

Salton
Sea

0   15   30
Miles

0   3,500   7,000
Feet

The City of La Quinta, "Gem of the Desert," is nestled near the Santa Rosa Mountains and is home to over 20 golf courses including the famous PGA West. The La Quinta Art Festival is held here and there is a quaint Old Town Village with shopping and dining nearby. This ride takes you past a number of beautiful golf courses and you can experience "The Cove" with its colorful southwest style houses and scenic views of the nearby Santa Rosa Mountains.

From Fritz Burns Community Park, start pedaling north on Avenida Bermudas. Soon you will pass by the delightful streets of La Quinta's Old Town Village on your right, a great place to get something to eat and meander after the ride.

Turn right on Calle Tampico and head past the library and Civic Center on your right. Curve left as the street changes to Park Avenue and you ride alongside Painted Cove. At Avenue 50 turn right and right again at Jefferson Street. Continue straight on this wide beautiful street and through the roundabout at Avenue 52 and continue to 54th Avenue. You can take a brief detour through PGA West straight ahead, see Options.

To continue the ride, turn left on 54th Avenue and head east to Madison Street and turn right. Follow Madison past the Griffin Ranch for 2 miles along the PGA West area to 58th Avenue and turn left. At Monroe turn left and pedal past several palm groves and the Palms Golf Club and PGA West again. Stay on Monroe for 3 miles and turn left on 52nd Avenue. Indio is to the east and north of here. Turn right on Madison Street then left on 50th Avenue.

Turn right on Jefferson Street and pass by Rancho La Quinta Country Club on your left. At Avenue 48 turn left and then left again on Washington Street. Turn right on Eisenhower Drive and follow it past La Quinta Resort and Club and turn right on Avenida Montezuma. Soon you begin an easy climb past many colorful southwest style houses with a view of the nearby Santa Rosa Mountains. The Fred Wolff Bear Creek Trail bike path is to your right along this route and every now and then a small ramada with a bench and water fountain await if you want to fill your bottle. You could also ride on that bike path to the "Top of the Cove" instead of the street. To follow the street, take a brief left on Calle Ensenada then the second right on Avenida Juarez, which turns into Avenida Montezuma.

Once at the "Top of the Cove" stay left onto Calle Tecate. You will pass by two Cove Oasis Trailheads on your right that provide access to a 114 acre natural open space area with hiking and mountain biking trails. See the Cove Oasis Trails ride. Curve left onto Avenida Bermudas and enjoy the nice downhill run back to Fritz Burns Community Park.

OPTIONS

When Jefferson meets 54th Avenue you can continue straight onto PGA Boulevard and do a 3 mile out and back through PGA West. You pass by Arnold Palmer, Pete Dye, PGA West, Jack Nicklaus Boulevard and Weiskopf before turning around.

OLD TOWN LA QUINTA

Old Town La Quinta is along Main Street south and east of the intersection of Avenida Bermudas and Calle Tampico. It offers a number of interesting shops, restaurants, and art galleries in an environment reminiscent of early California. You can extend the ride a bit by cruising on Old Town Lane, Main Street and a one way loop on Avenida la Fonda. Water fountains and benches mark the ends of Avenida la Fonda and Calle Estado one street farther south. La Quinta Village Park is just west of Avenida Bermudas on Avenida Montezuma.

GETTING THERE

From Highway 111 take Washington Boulevard south. Turn right on Avenue 52 then left on Avenida Bermudas. Park anywhere in or near Fritz Burns Community Park.

AMENITIES

Old Town La Quinta just north of the starting point is a great place to visit and get something to eat after the ride. You won't find big name establishments here but the charm of locally owned and operated shops. Water is available at several places on the Fred Wolff Bear Creek Trail bike path and at Fritz Burns Community Park.

Trip E3 - Cove Oasis Trails

Starting Point	Top of The Cove, La Quinta
Distance	2 to 5 miles depending on route
Elevation Gain/Loss	100'/100'
Riding Time	30–60 minutes depending on route
Difficulty	Easy, not technical
Road Conditions	Dirt trails
Season	Fall, Winter, Spring
Equipment	Mountain bike
Optional Topo Map	La Quinta, CA

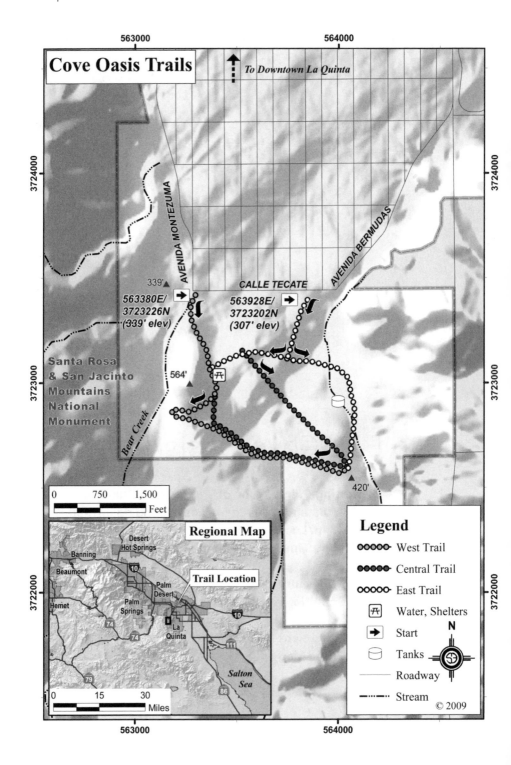

Cove Oasis Trails

To Downtown La Quinta

563000

564000

3724000

AVENIDA MONTEZUMA

AVENIDA BERMUDAS

339'

563380E/
3723226N
(339' elev)

CALLE TECATE

563928E/
3723202N
(307' elev)

Santa Rosa
& San Jacinto
Mountains
National
Monument

564'

Bear Creek

3723000

420'

0   750   1,500
Feet

Regional Map

Desert
Hot Springs

Banning

Beaumont

Palm
Desert

Trail Location

Hemet

Palm
Springs

La
Quinta

Salton
Sea

0   15   30
Miles

Legend

ooooo West Trail

●●●●● Central Trail

ooooo East Trail

🏕 Water, Shelters

➡ Start

🛢 Tanks

— Roadway

---- Stream

N

© 2009

3722000

La Quinta Cove is surrounded by a number of exclusive gated communities and country clubs. Once inside the cove, however, the colorful southwest style homes and beautiful landscaping take over. The rugged Santa Rosa Mountains provide a spectacular backdrop to the area. There is easy access to the surrounding recreational areas, including several dirt trails accessed from the Top of the Cove. On this ride you will explore a few of these trails in the Cove Oasis area, enjoy views of the nearby Santa Rosa Mountains, and you may get a chance to see a greater roadrunner or Gambel's quail recognized by its top knot.

There are two trailheads you can use to start this ride. Both provide access to the same trails and to Cove Oasis where you will find picnic tables, benches, and a water fountain. There are many routes you can take in this area, this ride describes several possible choices.

To reach Cove Oasis, head south from either starting point. It is 0.25 miles from the western trailhead. From the eastern trailhead take the first right to reach Cove Oasis in about 0.4 mile. The palm trees at Cove Oasis were donated to the City of La Quinta in 1996. They can grow to a height of 50-60 feet and only the females produce fruit.

From Cove Oasis head south and ride past the small hill on your right. You can turn right, and angle around and down the pile of rocks on your right, or head left and ride across the top of the dam. If you choose to go right, once around the rocks you can explore several trails including one along the top of the wash to the west. But note that the Bear Creek Oasis Trail in the wash to the west is closed from June 15 to September 30 to minimize impact to water access by bighorn sheep and other wildlife.

From the bottom of the dam a good choice is to head east along the base of the dam. You can climb back up the dam on the eastern end and take the trail north to the right of the tanks or follow the trail across the middle of the area heading to the right of Cove Oasis. As you can see, there are any number of ways you can link the various trails in Cove Oasis to create a new ride each time you ride here.

GETTING THERE

From Highway 111 take Washington Boulevard south. Turn right on Avenue 52 then left on Avenida Bermudas and follow it south until it curves west and becomes Calle Tecate. There are two trailheads, one near Avenida Ramirez with a dirt parking lot and one farther west by Avenida Madero where you can park on the street.

AMENITIES

La Quinta Old Town Village at the corner of Avenida Bermudas and Calle Tampico is a good place to get something to eat after the ride. You won't find big name establishments here but the charm of locally owned and operated shops.

Water is available at the ramada near the west trailhead and at Cove Oasis 0.25 miles on the trail.

Trip E4 - Indio Mural Tour

Starting Point	Smurr Street, Downtown Indio
Distance	4 miles
Elevation Gain/Loss	Flat
Riding Time	45 minutes
Difficulty	Easy, not technical
Road Conditions	City streets
Season	Fall, Winter, Spring
Equipment	Any bicycle
Optional Topo Map	Indio, CA

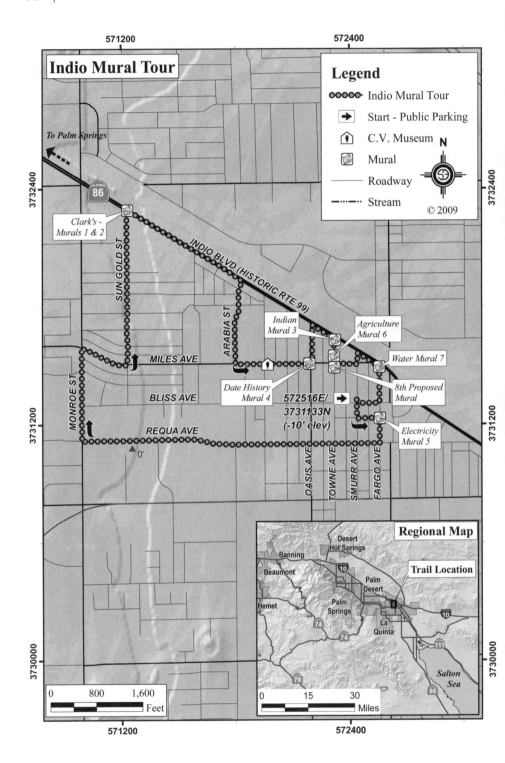

Indio Mural Tour

Legend

⊶⊶⊶ Indio Mural Tour

➡ Start - Public Parking

⬆ C.V. Museum

🖼 Mural

— Roadway

—·····— Stream

© 2009

N

To Palm Springs

86

Clark's - Murals 1 & 2

INDIO BLVD (HISTORIC RTE 99)

SUN GOLD ST

ARABIA ST

MONROE ST

MILES AVE

BLISS AVE

REQUA AVE

0'

Indian Mural 3

Date History Mural 4

572516E/ 3731133N (-10' elev)

Agriculture Mural 6

Water Mural 7

8th Proposed Mural

Electricity Mural 5

OASIS AVE

TOWNE AVE

SMURR AVE

FARGO AVE

0   800   1,600
Feet

Regional Map

Trail Location

Banning

Beaumont

Hemet

Desert Hot Springs

Palm Desert

Palm Springs

La Quinta

Salton Sea

10

74

74

79

10

111

86

0   15   30
Miles

In 1996 the Indio Chamber of Commerce embarked on a project to develop a number of historic murals to help revitalize the local economy and encourage pride and tourism as well as honor the cultural history of the area. Currently there are seven murals throughout the Old Town area with an eighth one planned soon with a goal of thirty. This easy ride takes you to each of the murals that will provide you with a glimpse into the history and development of the Coachella Valley.

But first a bit about historic Indio. Indio was a winter home for Native Americans who migrated from the surrounding mountains to the warmer desert floor and palm oases during the winter. In late 1800s the Southern Pacific Railroad established the "Indian Wells" distribution point and the first date palm shoots were imported from Algeria. The name of the town was changed to Indio in 1879. By 1920 Indio had become the date capital of the United States. General Patton took up residence in Hotel Indio and trained his troops nearby (see the Box Canyon Earthquake Route ride, which starts near the General George S. Patton Museum at Chiriaco Summit). Indio was the Coachella Valley's first incorporated city in 1930 and the All-American Canal began delivering much needed Colorado River water in 1948.

Today Indio describes itself as the City of Festivals. The International Tamale Festival is the first weekend in December followed by the Southwest Arts Festival and the National Date Festival plus many others. The Old Town Indio Streetfest runs the second Tuesday of each month from October to May. The two day Coachella Valley Music and Arts Festival in April is one of the best festivals around.

Start this ride at the Public Parking lot on Smurr Street just north of Bliss Avenue. Continue South on Smurr Street past the Indio Civic Center and turn left on Civic Center Drive. On the north wall of the former Imperial Irrigation District building on the southwest corner of Civic Center Drive and Fargo Street is Mural #5, the History of Electricity in Indio and the East Coachella Valley. The agricultural industry needed electric services to preserve the produce. From cold storage houses to electrical transport, the eastern Coachella was transformed.

Turn right on Fargo Street then right on Requa Avenue and enjoy the palm grove as you head to Monroe Street. Turn right on Miles and left on Sun Gold Street. At Indio Blvd on the historic Route 99 Clark's Truck Stop and General Store building are Mural #1, Transportation, on the west wall and Mural #2, Mary Ann's Bakery on the north wall. Mary Ann's Bakery of Thermal delivered baked goods to Indio. The interesting historical building is worth exploring inside and out (pay particular attention to one of the plaques on the front).

Continue southeast on Indio Blvd, also known as Historic Route 99, which once extended from Canada to the Mexico border. It became the busiest truck route in the country and was called the Main Street of California. It slowly disappeared as the freeway systems expanded starting in the 1960s. An effort to revitalize Route 99 is underway.

Turn right on Arabia Street and pass by Miles Park. Restrooms and water are available here. This is also an alternate starting point for the ride. Turn left on Miles Avenue and notice Deglet Noor Street as you head past the Coachella Valley Museum and Cultural Center, which is worth visiting after the ride. Deglet Noor is a date originally from Algeria and Tunisia and grown in the valley.

On your right at the corner of Miles Avenue and Oasis Street is Mural #4, The History of the Date Industry in the Coachella Valley. The date industry started in the 1800s with a few palm shoots and has expanded rapidly since then. The most common commercial variety is Deglet Noor but more recent varieties like Medjool from French Morocco are gaining popularity. The female date blossoms are pollinated by hand and the trees grow from 20 to 100 feet high. You must try some after the ride (see Amenities).

After your fill of date history turn left on Oasis Street, right on Indio Blvd and at Towne Street on the north wall of the old Yellow Mart store is Mural #3, Life in an Indian Village Circa 1700. This mural was sponsored by the Cabazon Band of Mission Indians, and depicts an Indian Village in the 1700s that was actually a little east of the building.

Continue south on Towne Street and immediately on your right before Miles Avenue on the wall of the Yellow Mart Mall building is Mural #6, Agriculture in the Coachella Valley.

The proposed site of Mural #8 is just south of this point on Civic Center Mall. Turn left on Miles Avenue and ride through a nice one-way street with interesting shops. Turn left at Smurr St past the Indio Chamber of Commerce and then right on Indio Blvd and then quickly right on Fargo Street for Mural #7, The History of Water in the Coachella Valley. Located on the south side of the Twisters Building housing the Indio Performing Arts Center, it depicts the harvesting and use of water in this area.

Continue south on Fargo Street then right on Bliss Avenue and right again on Smurr Street to return to the start.

GETTING THERE

From I-10 exit at Jackson Street and head south. Turn right on Civic Center Drive then right on Smurr Street to the Public Parking just north of Bliss Avenue. From Highway 111 (Avenue 46) head north on Smurr Street to the Public Parking just north of Bliss Avenue.

AMENITIES

You can try date samples and enjoy a date shake after your bike ride at Shields Date Garden, 80-225 Highway 111 in Indio and Oasis Date Gardens, 59-111 Highway 111 in Thermal.

Trip E5 - Terra Lago Tour

Starting Point	Golf Center Parkway, north Indio
Distance	3 or 4.5 miles
Elevation Gain/Loss	Flat
Riding Time	30 minutes
Difficulty	Easy, not technical
Road Conditions	City streets
Season	Fall, Winter, Spring
Equipment	Any bicycle
Optional Topo Map	Indio, CA

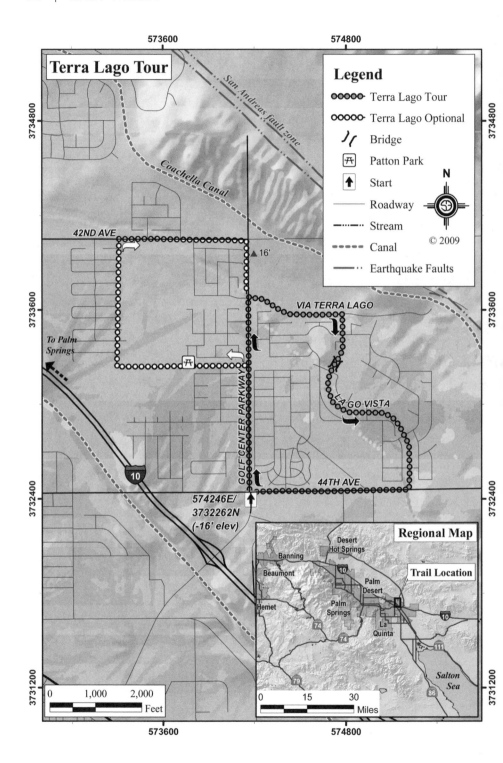

Terra Lago Tour

Legend

⬭⬭⬭⬭⬭ Terra Lago Tour

○○○○○ Terra Lago Optional

)(Bridge

🪧 Patton Park

⬆ Start

—— Roadway

—··—·· Stream

- - - - Canal

—— ·· Earthquake Faults

N

© 2009

San Andreas fault zone

Coachella Canal

42ND AVE

▲ 16'

VIA TERRA LAGO

To Palm Springs

🪧

GOLF CENTER PARKWAY

LAGO VISTA

10

44TH AVE

574246E/ 3732262N (-16' elev)

Regional Map

Trail Location

Desert Hot Springs

Banning

Beaumont

10

Palm Desert

Hemet

Palm Springs

74

74

La Quinta

10

111

79

Salton Sea

86

0   1,000   2,000
Feet

0   15   30
Miles

This short ride will show you what some describe as Coachella Valley's latest oxymoron: a master-planned lake-oriented desert community in north Indio. You will ride past beautiful homes surrounding large bodies of water complete with sailboats and Italian-style bridges. This may be the new style of innovative developments in the valley and is a great way to spend some time on a nice sunny day.

Terra Lago, which in Italian means land of lakes, is built around a 20-acre waterway. Small sailboats, kayaks, and small electric watercraft are allowed for residents and their guests. But don't wear your swim suit on this ride; swimming is not allowed.

Start riding north on wide, four-lane Golf Center Parkway with mesquite trees enhancing the landscape. Continue north to Terra Lago Parkway. Turn right and enjoy the lakes and stream on your right, a preview of coming attractions. Turn right on Lago Vista and head into the heart of Terra Lago. Climb up the arched Italian-style bridge. You might want to pause here and enjoy the master-planned waterfront community and magnificent lake in all directions.

Glide your way down the bridge and continue on curving, nicely landscaped Lago Vista. There are several side streets you could explore, some leading to arms of the lake. Continue on Lago Vista to Avenue 44 and turn right and pedal past Aliante and Rancho Casa Blanca and back to Golf Center Parkway and your car.

OPTIONS

To extend the ride 1.5 miles and visit George S. Patton Park, from Golf Center Parkway turn left on Avenue 43 and head 0.25 mile to the park on your right. Continue west to Calhoun Street and turn right. At Avenue 42 turn right and right again on Golf Center Parkway. A sign on the left indicates a City of Indio future park site. Turn left on Terra Lago Parkway to continue the ride into Terra Lago.

GETTING THERE

From I-10 exit at Golf Center Parkway head north. Park just north of Avenue 44.

AMENITIES

You can try date samples and enjoy a date shake after your bike ride at Shields Date Garden, 80-225 Highway 111 in Indio and Oasis Date Gardens, 59-111 Highway 111 in Thermal.

Trip E6 - Painted Canyon

Starting Point	Box Canyon Road near Mecca
Distance	9 miles out and back
Elevation Gain/Loss	600'/40' one way, 3.5% average grade
Riding Time	2.5 hours
Difficulty	Moderate, not technical
Road Conditions	Dirt road, loose sand in places
Season	Fall, Winter, Spring
Equipment	Mountain bike
Optional Topo Map	Mecca, CA

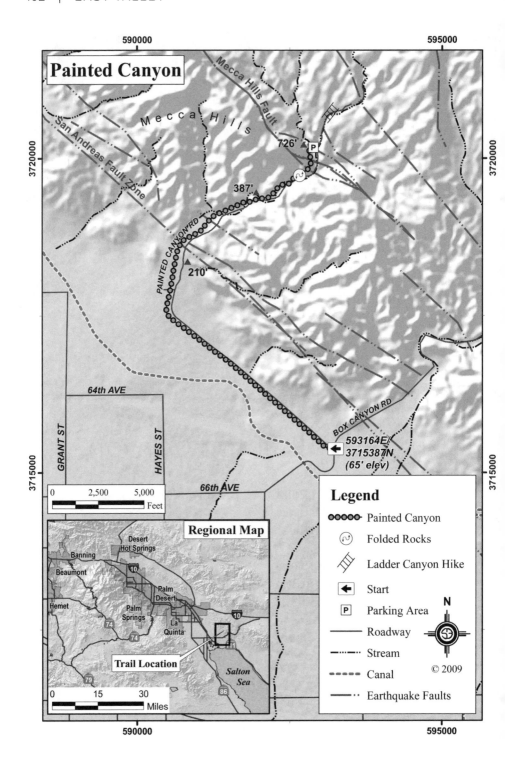

Painted Canyon

Mecca Hills Fault

Mecca Hills

San Andreas Fault Zone

726'

P

387'

PAINTED CANYON RD

210'

64th AVE

GRANT ST

HAYES ST

BOX CANYON RD

593164E/
3715387N
(65' elev)

0   2,500   5,000
Feet

66th AVE

Regional Map

Desert
Hot Springs

Banning

Beaumont

10

Palm
Desert

Hemet

Palm
Springs

La
Quinta

10

74

74

Trail Location

Salton
Sea

79

86

0   15   30
Miles

Legend

⊙⊙⊙⊙⊙ Painted Canyon

⟲ Folded Rocks

⫽ Ladder Canyon Hike

← Start

P Parking Area

— Roadway

—···— Stream

----- Canal

—··— Earthquake Faults

N

© 2009

The Mecca Hills, about 40 miles southeast of Palm Springs, is a unique and colorful area of sedimentary badlands uplifted and folded by the San Andreas Fault Zone running through the area. Painted Canyon is a narrow, high-walled canyon that reminds one of an artist's palette of pastel pink, red, brown, gray, and green that are best seen in afternoon light. This ride will take you through the canyon where you can experience the beautiful canyon walls first hand. The road is called a "cherry stem" or a legal corridor for vehicles into the Mecca Hills Wilderness.

Start pedaling northwest on the graded gravel road. The sign indicates this is the Mecca Hills Wilderness Area. The road is fairly flat for the first 1.5 miles and then slowly starts climbing. The hills to your right start to give a hint of the colors that await you farther up the canyon. You will notice lots of cat-claw acacia, Palo Verde, and smoke trees in the area. Around 3 miles the canyon walls begin to narrow as the road curves northeast. Watch for sandy sections and try to stay on firmer ground and avoid vehicles trying to do the same.

At 4 miles a highly folded and colorful wall appears on your left. Mineral deposits in the rock account for the various beautiful colors. The road continues to wind its way through the canyon with new sights at every turn. When you reach the parking area this is the turnaround point. Bikes are not allowed beyond here but there are some nice slot canyons you can hike. See Options.

OPTIONS

This ride can be an out and back or you can have a friend in a 4WD vehicle drop you off at the top of the canyon and you can pedal downhill and enjoy the wonderful canyon the easy way.

Ladder Canyon is an optional hike you can do (bikes not allowed). It is located on the left a short distance up the right canyon fork after the parking area (look for the sign on the right pointing left). The narrow twisty canyon with a number of dry waterfalls is made accessible by several aluminum ladders, the longest about 20 feet. This is a highly recommended side trip if you have a way to secure your bike and are not afraid of heights. Check the ladders before climbing them.

GETTING THERE

Take Highway 111 to Mecca and exit left at 66th Avenue. It curves right and becomes Hammond Avenue then turn left on 66th or Box Canyon Road. Follow Box Canyon Road about 5 miles passing over the Coachella Canal to Painted

Canyon Road on your left. Park off the road here. You can shorten the ride by parking closer to the mouth of the canyon or do a one-way downhill ride by having a friend drive you to the end of the canyon and riding back. A 4WD vehicle is highly recommended since there is loose sand in places.

AMENITIES

A small store and several restaurants are available in the town of Mecca. You can try date samples and enjoy a date shake after your bike ride at Oasis Date Gardens, 59-111 Highway 111 in Thermal.

Open camping is available in Box Canyon and in other BLM, non-wilderness areas. Park your vehicle outside any wilderness boundaries and in previously disturbed sites.

Trip E7 - Little Box Canyon Trail

Starting Point	Box Canyon Road east of Mecca
Distance	6 miles
Elevation Gain/Loss	300'/300'
Riding Time	1.5 hours
Difficulty	Moderate, not technical
Road Conditions	Dirt road, loose sand in places
Season	Fall, Winter, Spring
Equipment	Mountain bike
Optional Topo Map	Mortmar, CA

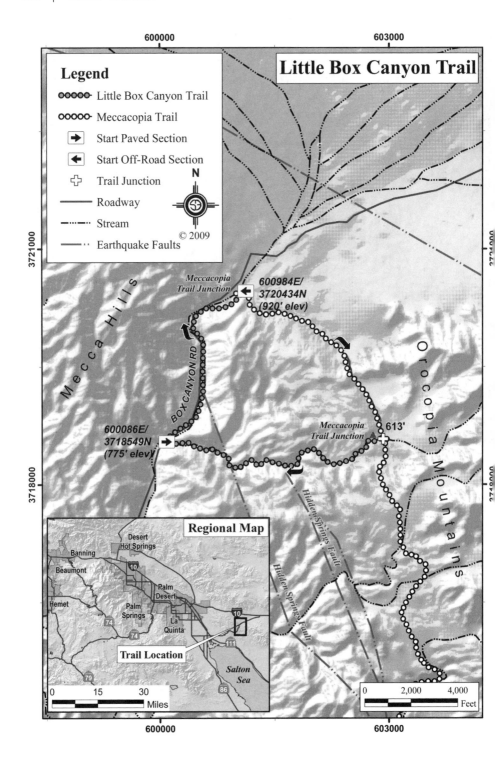

Little Box Canyon Trail

Legend

ooooo— Little Box Canyon Trail

ooooo— Meccacopia Trail

[→] Start Paved Section

[←] Start Off-Road Section

⊹ Trail Junction

—— Roadway

—·····— Stream

—— ·· Earthquake Faults

© 2009

N

Meccacopia Trail Junction [←] 600984E/ 3720434N (920' elev)

Meccacopia Trail Junction ⊹ 613'

600086E/ 3718549N (775' elev) [→]

BOX CANYON RD

Mecca Hills

Orocopia Mountains

Hidden Springs Fault

Hidden Springs Fault

Regional Map

Desert Hot Springs

Banning

Beaumont

10

Palm Desert

Hemet

Palm Springs

74

74

La Quinta

10

Trail Location

111

Salton Sea

79

86

0   15   30
Miles

0   2,000   4,000
Feet

Little Box Canyon is a small, narrow-walled scenic canyon on the eastern edge of the Mecca Hills. This easy ride starts on the Meccacopia Trail, part of the BLM Special Recreational Management Area that consists of the Mecca Hills and the Orocopia Mountains Wilderness areas, and ends in the Mecca Hills. The heart of Little Box Canyon is within the wilderness area and provides nice views into the colorful eastern Mecca Hills.

The ride starts at the northern end of Box Canyon before the Shavers Well monument. Ride northeast 1.6 miles on the pavement past the Shavers Well monument to the Meccacopia Trail sign on your right. Head east on the Meccacopia Trail through a small sandy canyon. Soon the trail climbs onto an open rocky area and provides great views of the Cottonwood Mountains to the north, The Orocopia Mountains to the east, and the Mecca Hills to the west. I-10 is just a silent line of cars and trucks in the distance. Soon the road climbs sharply over a small rise and opens into a wide valley. Many limited-use trails crisscross this area.

At mile 2 you encounter the signed trail to Little Box Canyon. Turn right and start heading into the canyon. The road winds around through the canyon, usually in the wash, providing nice views of the alluvial hills. Several trails head left and right into limited-use areas where you must stay on existing routes if you want to explore a little. Once you pass the Wilderness sign you must stay in the wash bottom for the next mile.

Soon nice views west to the colorful, banded Mecca Hills peak around hills in the wash. The road continues to wind its way through the canyon with new sights at every turn. After 2.3 miles in the canyon you reach the pavement at Box Canyon Road and your car.

GETTING THERE

Take Highway 111 to Mecca and exit left at 66th Avenue. It curves right and becomes Hammond Avenue then turn left on 66th or Box Canyon Road. Follow Box Canyon Road about 11 miles passing over the Coachella Canal and through most of Box Canyon to the sign for Little Box Canyon on your right before the Shavers Well monument. Park off the road here.

You can also take I-10 east to Cottonwood Springs/Box Canyon exit before Chiriaco Summit, turn right and drive 8.5 miles to the Little Box Canyon Trail sign on your left not far past the Shavers Well monument.

AMENITIES

A small store and several restaurants are available in the town of Mecca. You can try date samples and enjoy a date shake after your bike ride at Oasis Date Gardens, 59-111 Highway 111 in Thermal.

Open camping is available in Box Canyon and in other BLM, non-wilderness areas. Park your vehicle outside any wilderness boundaries and in previously disturbed sites.

Trip E8 - Meccacopia Trail

Starting Point	Box Canyon Road east of Mecca
Distance	11 miles one-way
Elevation Gain/Loss	220'/1180'
Riding Time	3–4 hours
Difficulty	Moderate, not technical
Road Conditions	Dirt road, loose sand in places
Season	Fall, Winter, Spring
Equipment	Mountain bike
Optional Topo Map	Mortmar, CA

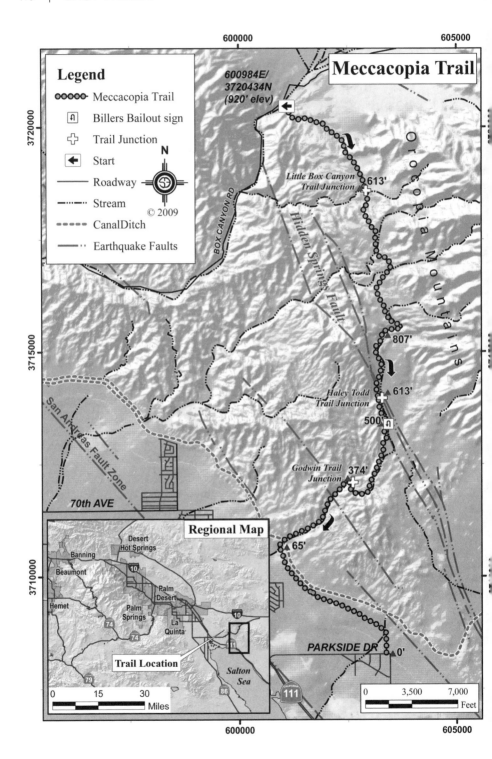

Meccacopia Trail

Legend

⊙⊙⊙⊙⊙ Meccacopia Trail

🄽 Billers Bailout sign

✢ Trail Junction

← Start

—— Roadway

—··—··— Stream

----- CanalDitch

——·· Earthquake Faults

© 2009

N

600984E/
3720434N
(920' elev) ←

Little Box Canyon
Trail Junction 613'

BOX CANYON RD

Hidden Springs Fault

Orocopia Mountains

807'

613'

Haley Todd
Trail Junction 500' 🄽

Godwin Trail 374'
Junction

San Andreas Fault Zone

70th AVE

65'

Regional Map

Desert
Hot Springs

Banning

Beaumont

Palm
Desert

Hemet

Palm
Springs

La
Quinta

10

10

Trail Location

Salton
Sea

74

74

79

86

111

0   15   30
Miles

PARKSIDE DR 0'

0   3,500   7,000
Feet

Meccacopia is a name given to the BLM Special Recreational Management Area that consists of the Mecca Hills and the Orocopia Mountains Wilderness areas. This area implements a number of vehicle loop routes but tries to minimize their intrusion into the surrounding desert wilderness. The Meccacopia Trail is one of these routes and is a fun trail to ride that will take you past some of the wilderness areas as well as provide a great view into the Mecca Hills badlands and the Salton Sea beyond.

The ride starts at the northern end of Box Canyon just past the Shavers Well monument. Head east on the Meccacopia Trail through a small sandy canyon. Soon the trail climbs onto an open rocky plateau and provides great views of the Cottonwood Mountains to the north, the Orocopia Mountains to the east and the Mecca Hills to the west. Cars and trucks on I-10 in the distance are too far away to spoil the quiet. Soon the road climbs sharply over a small rise and you begin to enjoy the flat valley here and then the generally downhill trend of the trail. Many limited-use trails crisscross this area.

At mile 2 you pass the Little Box Canyon junction on your right. This is the last place to bail out (see Options). The trail then starts to head downhill and the canyon narrows to a mere seven feet wide for a short distance. Palo Verde and mesquite bushes highlight the nearby landscape. About 2.5 miles past the Little Box Canyon junction is a nice Salton Sea view to the south. In another mile a sign for the Haley Todd Ridge Trail beckons you on the right. Leave your bike here and climb the steep trail to the top of the hill. This is an awesome view west into the Mecca Hills badlands. The route below you into the badlands and through sandy washes is frequented mainly by motorcycles and should join up with the Meccacopia Trail farther south, but is not covered here.

Soon you will pass the Billers Bailout sign on your left and then a Wilderness boundary sign. When you near the east-west wash ahead a Meccacopia trail sign indicates you should stay straight. At the wash stay right and make a few turns in the narrowing canyon, which then opens up into a larger canyon. Go left past the Godwin and McLane Trails on your right. You are now in the main wash heading west and an area frequented by RV's and off-road vehicles. Sections of the wash can be sandy so look for hard-packed areas. At roughly 15 miles from the start you will cross over the Coachella Canal. Turn left by the control gate and stay on the road above and paralleling the canal. A number of dirt roads exit this route. Find a major one and head roughly southeast and then south. You should come out near Desertaire and Parkside Drive where your vehicle is waiting. Check your GPS reading for your parked car to make sure you are heading in the correct direction.

OPTIONS

You can bail out of this ride at Little Box Canyon at 2 miles. Head right for 2.3 miles back to Box Canyon Road and turn right to return 1.6 miles on the pavement to your car for a total ride distance of 6 miles. See the Little Box Canyon Trail ride for a description of this route.

GETTING THERE

This ride requires a car shuttle. To leave the first car, take Highway 111 past Mecca and turn left onto Parkside when you see the Salton Sea State Recreation Area sign on your right. Turn left on Desertaire and park near the end of the paved road. If you carry a GPS (recommended), save this waypoint: 11S 603413 3708321 or wherever you park your car. To reach the starting point take Highway 111 back to Mecca and exit east at 66th Avenue. It curves right and becomes Hammond Avenue then turn left on 66th or Box Canyon Road. Follow Box Canyon Road about 7 miles passing over the Coachella Canal and through most of Box Canyon to the sign on the right for the Meccacopia Trail. Park off the road here to start the ride.

AMENITIES

A small store and several restaurants are available in the town of Mecca. You can try date samples and enjoy a date shake after your bike ride at Oasis Date Gardens, 59-111 Highway 111 in Thermal.

Open camping is available in Box Canyon and in other BLM, non-wilderness areas. Park your vehicle outside any wilderness boundaries and in previously disturbed sites.

Trip E9 - Box Canyon Earthquake Route

Starting Point	Chiriaco Summit, I-10
Distance	24 miles one-way
Elevation Gain/Loss	20'/1900'
Riding Time	1.5 hours
Difficulty	Easy, all downhill, not technical
Road Conditions	Paved roads
Season	Fall, Winter, Spring
Equipment	Any bicycle
Optional Topo Maps	Hayfield, Cottonwood Spring, Mortmar, and Mecca, CA

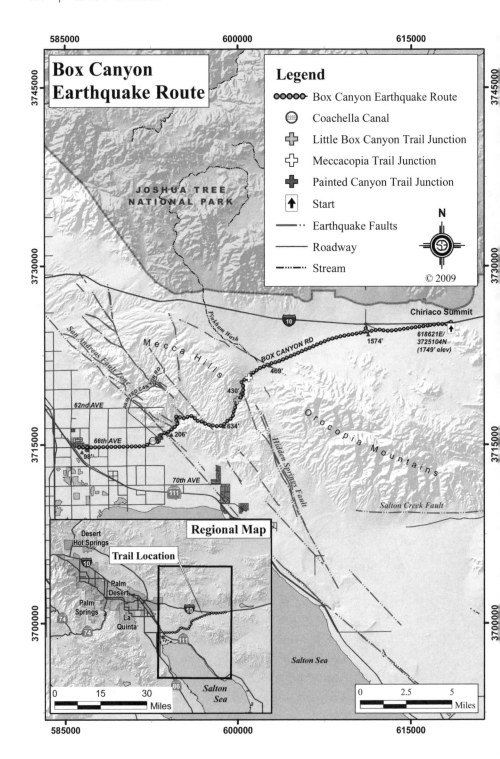

Box Canyon Earthquake Route

Legend

ᴏᴏᴏᴏᴏ Box Canyon Earthquake Route

⬤ Coachella Canal

✚ Little Box Canyon Trail Junction

✚ Meccacopia Trail Junction

✚ Painted Canyon Trail Junction

↑ Start

—·· Earthquake Faults

— Roadway

—·—·· Stream

© 2009

JOSHUA TREE NATIONAL PARK

Chiriaco Summit

618621E/
3725104N
(1749' elev)

1574'

BOX CANYON RD

Pinkham Wash

Mecca Hills

San Andreas Fault Zone

PAINTED CANYON RD

469'

430'

634'

206'

62nd AVE

66th AVE

98th

70th AVE

111

Orocopia Mountains

Hidden Springs Fault

Salton Creek Fault

Regional Map

Trail Location

Desert Hot Springs

10

Palm Desert

Palm Springs

74

La Quinta

74

10

111

86

Salton Sea

Salton Sea

0   15   30
Miles

0   2.5   5
Miles

The Mecca Hills are a colorful badlands of uplifted, twisted and folded sedimentary rocks and narrow canyons that are a result of action along the San Andreas Fault zone. The San Andreas Fault begins south of the Salton Sea and extends roughly 600 miles north through California. Box Canyon is one of these colorful canyons that you can explore on this ride. We start at Chiriaco Summit near where General George S. Patton in 1942 trained a million men to endure the desert conditions similar to what they would find in the Sahara Desert in Northern Africa. He set up Camp Young 1 mile east and it lasted until 1944 when the Allies declared victory in the Sahara. A memorial museum with tanks and other artifacts was created here in 1945. In the 1960s I-10 bypassed Highway 60 through Box Canyon and now it is a quiet place to ride.

From Chiriaco Summit, ride over I-10 and follow Pinto Road west as it slowly descends paralleling I-10. As you near Box Canyon Road exiting from I-10 stay left at the next junction and then you will join Box Canyon Road shortly. There may be a couple of short sections of gravel, which are easy to cross.

Follow Box Canyon as it descends through the desert with nice views to the west and south. After about 6.5 miles as you begin to enter Box Canyon you will pass a sign on the left marking the Meccacopia Trail, a great route for a mountain bike that travels between the Mecca and Orocopia Mountains. See the Meccacopia Trail trip.

Soon you pass a monument for Shavers Well on the right and about 1.5 miles past Meccacopia Trail the Little Box Canyon Trail is on your left. This off-road route joins the Meccacopia Trail and also is a ride in this book.

Continue through the canyon and it begins to open up into an area of wildly deformed, uplifted, and tilted sandstone beds. This is the San Andreas Fault Zone. The San Andreas Fault is a transform fault where opposite sides of the fault slide past one another at a couple of inches a year. Too slow to sit and watch, but you can see the results as rocks on each side crumble and deform into the hills around you.

At about 19 miles the canyon opens up and you should have a great view of the Salton Sea in the distance. At mile 20 you pass by Painted Canyon Road on your right, another canyon with a beautiful artist palette of colors in the folded rocks (see the Painted Canyon ride). The wash on your left immediately past Painted Canyon Road heads to the Godwin Trail, which joins the Meccacopia Trail. Shortly after that the road curves right and then up and over the Coachella Canal. Just past the canal is sea level and you continue your quick descent though citrus and grape vines past Johnson Road to your waiting car, which is about 100 feet below sea level.

GETTING THERE

This ride is best done as a car shuttle or to be dropped off at Chiriaco Summit and picked up at the end in Mecca. For the car shuttle, park one car on 66th Avenue in Mecca. To get there take Highway 111 to Mecca and exit left at 66th Avenue. It curves right and becomes Hammond Avenue then turn left on 66th or Box Canyon Road. Follow 66th a short distance past the main part of Mecca and park along the road. Then take Highway 111 to I-10 east to Chiriaco Summit and park the second car on Chiriaco Road or this is the drop-off point. You can shorten the ride by 4.5 miles by parking at Cottonwood Springs/Box Canyon before Chiriaco Summit. But you will miss the George S. Patton museum. Of course you can also drive up Box Canyon Road and park the second car at Chiriaco Summit, but that would spoil the surprise of the canyon.

AMENITIES

A small store and several restaurants are available in the town of Mecca. You can try date samples and enjoy a date shake after your bike ride at Oasis Date Gardens, 59-111 Highway 111 in Thermal.

Open camping is available in Box Canyon and in other BLM, non-wilderness areas. Park your vehicle outside any wilderness boundaries and in previously disturbed sites.

Trip M1 - Pinyon Flat Ride

Starting Point	Pinyon Flat Campground, Highway 74
Distance	6 miles
Elevation Gain/Loss	540'/540' – 3% average uphill grade
Riding Time	1.5 hours
Difficulty	Easy, not technical
Road Conditions	Dirt roads, small paved section
Season	Year-round, but can be hot in summer
Equipment	Mountain bike
Optional Topo Map	Toro Peak, CA

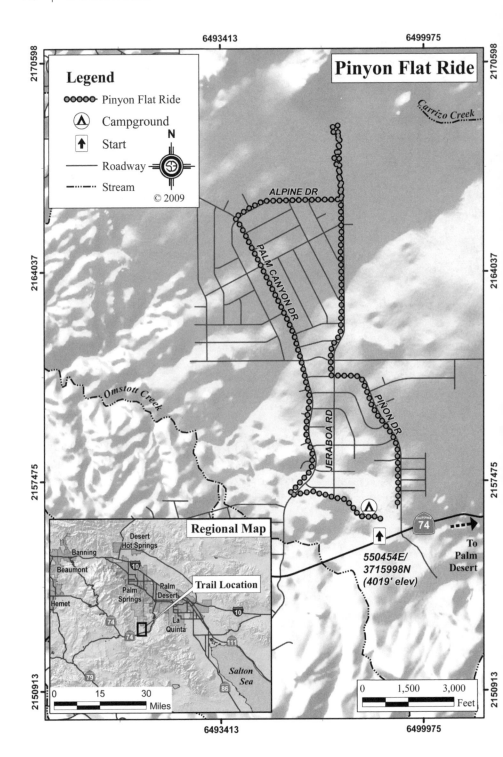

Legend
- ○○○○○ Pinyon Flat Ride
- Ⓐ Campground
- ⬆ Start
- —— Roadway
- —··—··— Stream

N

© 2009

Pinyon Flat Ride

6493413

6499975

2170598

2164037

2157475

2150913

Carrizo Creek

ALPINE DR

PALM CANYON DR

Omstott Creek

JERABOA RD

PINON DR

Ⓐ

74

To
Palm
Desert

550454E/
3715998N
(4019' elev)

Regional Map

Desert
Hot Springs

Banning

Beaumont

Palm
Springs

Palm
Desert

Hemet

Trail Location

La
Quinta

10

10

111

74

74

79

86

Salton
Sea

0   15   30
Miles

0   1,500   3,000
Feet

Pinyon Flat is a nice area to enjoy a relatively flat, easy bike ride on dirt roads through quiet mountain neighborhoods. It is part of the San Bernardino National Forest and lies between the San Jacinto Mountains to the north and the Santa Rosa Mountains to the south. The ride starts at Pinyon Flat Campground at 4000' which will be cooler than the desert floor in warmer months but can still be pretty hot. This area is a great base camp for a number of other great rides and hiking trails in the area. The Palm Canyon – Pinyon Flat Loop ride also starts here.

Ride into the campground and circle either way on the road to campsite 11. The trail starts on the backside of the parking area for this camping spot. Head west on the trail and stay generally west as you come to any junctions. Shortly you parallel a fence and turn right and then left past the fence. When you reach Palm Canyon Drive turn right and start the slow easy uphill ride alongside the many eclectic homes. Some seem to be in a perpetual state of development.

The developer of this area must have longed for higher climes given the names of some of the roads: Saint Moritz Drive, Glacier Pass, and Matterhorn View. Although at 4000' there must be some snow that falls here now and then. Turn right at Alpine Drive and follow this to Jeraboa Road. Turn left and continue climbing toward Asbestos Mountain ahead of you. There can be loose sand in places so look for firmer areas to ride. At the junction you can head left or right and continue for a short distance. Turn around and head back down when you want to continue the ride. Note that left at the junction takes you through a fun roller coaster ride downhill and eventually joins Palm Canyon Drive. But that is private property behind the gate on Palm Canyon Drive so it is best to turn around near the junction.

Once heading back down Jeraboa Road turn left at Pinyon Drive. It climbs briefly and then starts a gentle downhill ride back to the campground. The last quarter of a mile is paved.

GETTING THERE

From the junction of Highway 111 and Highway 74 in Palm Desert drive 15.5 miles to Pinyon Drive and the Pinyon Flat Campground on your right. Turn right and park off the road here outside the campground.

AMENITIES

Paradise Corner Café is a nice place to eat after the ride at the junction of Highway 74 and Highway 371. Water and restrooms are available at the Pinyon Flat Campground.

Camping is available at Pinyon Flat Campground where this ride starts. Hurkey Creek Park is four miles southeast of Mountain Center on Highway 74. A number of primitive campgrounds at yellow post sites are also available off of Apple Canyon Road, on Thomas Mountain Ridge, and in the Garner Valley area and require a Forest Adventure Pass.

Trip M2 - Palm Canyon – Pinyon Flat Loop

Starting Point	Pinyon Flat Campground, Highway 74
Distance	11 miles: 8 dirt, 3 paved
Elevation Gain/Loss	2300'/2300' – 4% average uphill grade
Riding Time	3.5 hours
Difficulty	Difficult, technical
Road Conditions	Dirt trails, paved road
Season	Year-round, but can be hot in summer
Equipment	Mountain bike, extra inner tubes
Optional Topo Map	Toro Peak, CA

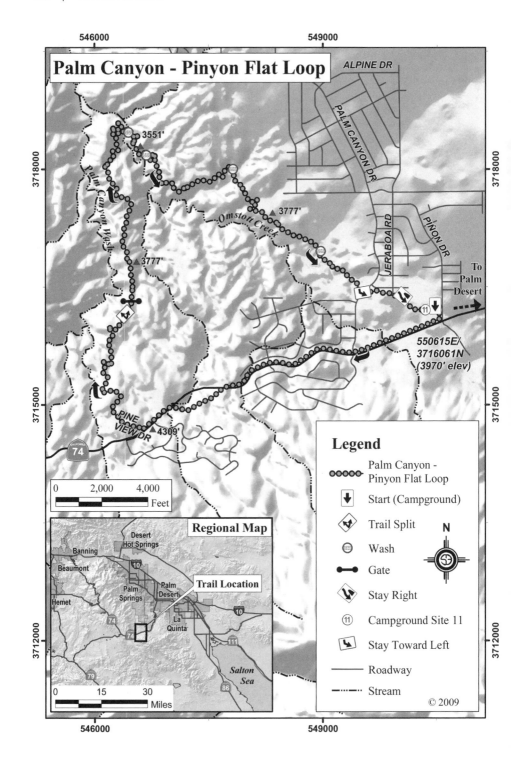

Palm Canyon - Pinyon Flat Loop

ALPINE DR

PALM CANYON DR

3551'

Palm Canyon Wash

Omston Creek

3777'

3777'

JERABOARD

PINON DR

To
Palm
Desert

550615E/
3716061N
(3970' elev)

PINE
VIEW DR

4309'

74

0   2,000   4,000
Feet

Regional Map

Desert
Hot Springs

Banning

Beaumont

10

Palm
Springs

Palm
Desert

Trail Location

Hemet

74

La
Quinta

10

74

111

Salton
Sea

79

86

0   15   30
Miles

Legend

Palm Canyon -
Pinyon Flat Loop

Start (Campground)

Trail Split

N

Wash

Gate

Stay Right

Campground Site 11

Stay Toward Left

Roadway

Stream

© 2009

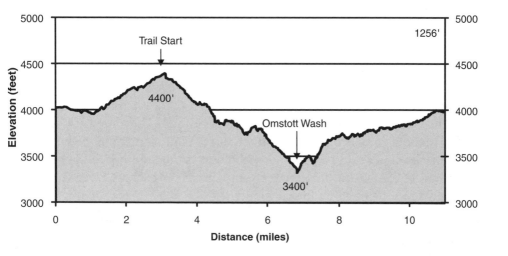

Pinyon Flat is located at 4000' on the northern slope of the Santa Rosa Mountains encircled by the small settlements of Alpine, Pinyon Pines, and Spring Crest. This ride starts in Pinyon Flat and descends into the upper reaches of Palm Canyon that divides the San Jacinto Mountains from the Santa Rosa Mountains and flows all the way to Palm Springs. Various flavors of Palm Canyon rides are described as epic due to their narrow, sometimes rocky, and cactus lined single track. This ride has a bit of all of that but at only 11 miles long you can get the epic flavor without the huge time commitment of the longer rides.

Since you will encounter cactus encroaching on your airspace it is best to ride with some friends and carry several tubes and a patch kit or use a slime-type product in your tubes. The ride starts by the Pinyon Flat Campground at 4000', which will be cooler than the desert floor in warmer months but can still be pretty hot.

From Pinyon Drive start pedaling west on Highway 74. You head generally downhill for 0.75 mile and then start the 2 mile 4% uphill grade to Pineview Road. There are a few trails that parallel the pavement in places but it is faster to stay on the road, just watch for cars. Turn right on Pineview Road and in 0.2 mile the road ends. Head straight on what used to be a 4WD road and at the junction stay right. The trail winds back and forth through chaparral and soon you start descending.

At 4.4 miles the trail descends quickly and you come to a four way junction. A Palm Canyon Trail sign 4E01, which might not be standing upright, shows the canyon bottom route to the left and the ridge top route straight ahead. Stay straight for the ridge to avoid the sandy wash below. The trail quickly starts climbing and comes to a gate at 4.5 miles. Make sure you close the gate after passing through.

The trail is on a double track for a short distance with great views into the canyon below. The trail then begins a wonderful run with ups and downs and back and forth between the ridge top and the side of the hill. At 5.6 miles you start hugging the west side of the ridge looking down into the canyon on your left and to the mountains north. Very soon the trail starts descending and you can see switchbacks on a south facing slope heading east and down into the canyon to your right as well as the single track south out of the canyon. Soon you will be blasting down the trail now in your sights.

From here the trail descends quickly, contouring and switch-backing on the hillside as you make your way down to Omstott Creek. Watch for cacti invading the trail and the occasional fragrant lavender plant brushing you. If you look southeast, partway down the slope you can see the switchbacks you will soon be riding heading back up to Pinyon Flat.

At 6.7 miles after some fairly sharp switchbacks you enter Omstott Creek wash. In the spring you may see water here and lots of lavender, Indian Paintbrush, and mallow. Folded metamorphic rock with white bands lines the wash. A small trail marker, sometimes on the ground, marks the trail on your left heading deeper north into Palm Canyon. For this ride, head slightly down wash and find the trail on the right heading up the bank and southward. The trail switchbacks up this small canyon, curves around the hillside, and drops down to a wash at 7.2 miles just before the big switchbacks out of the canyon.

The switchbacks are sharp and steep as you near the top and may require you to push your bike in a few places. Once at the top the trail hugs the side of the ridge above the wash. The trail then curves southeast and then east, providing great views south to the Santa Rosa Mountain ridge. You parallel a wash for awhile and then cross it at 8.6 miles. Head up the trail on the other side and the next mile or so is through an area that can be described as magical. The trail rolls up and down and winds its way through ribbonwood trees.

The trail crosses two washes and soon you are back in civilization as you pass by a nearby house. When you spot a brown sign with no markings on it and the back of a brown trail marker you are at Palm Canyon Road at 11 miles. Cross the road and continue on the trail directly opposite. When you encounter another brown trail marker stay to the left not right as it indicates. At another junction stay left on the more major trail. If you encounter a fence stay to the right of it and then right at the next junction to exit at campsite 11 or somewhere near the entrance to Pinyon Flat Campground. Turn right on the camp road to return to your car.

GETTING THERE

From the junction of Highway 111 and Highway 74 in Palm Desert drive 15.5 miles to Pinyon Drive and the Pinyon Flat Campground on your right. Turn right and park off the road here outside the campground.

AMENITIES

Paradise Corner Café is a nice place to eat after the ride at the junction of Highway 74 and Highway 371. Water and restrooms are available at the Pinyon Flat Campground.

Camping is available at Pinyon Flat Campground where this ride starts. Hurkey Creek Park is four miles southeast of Mountain Center on Highway 74. A number of primitive campgrounds at yellow post sites are also available off of Apple Canyon Road, on Thomas Mountain Ridge, and in the Garner Valley area and require a Forest Adventure Pass.

Trip M3 - Sawmill Trail

Starting Point	Santa Rosa Road, Highway 74
Distance	16 miles out and back (optional exit via Mount Santa Rosa Road)
Elevation Gain/Loss	3850'/3850' – 8% average grade
Riding Time	4–5 hours
Difficulty	Strenuous, technical
Road Conditions	Dirt road and trail
Season	Late spring, summer, early fall
Equipment	Mountain bike
Optional Topo Map	Toro Peak, CA

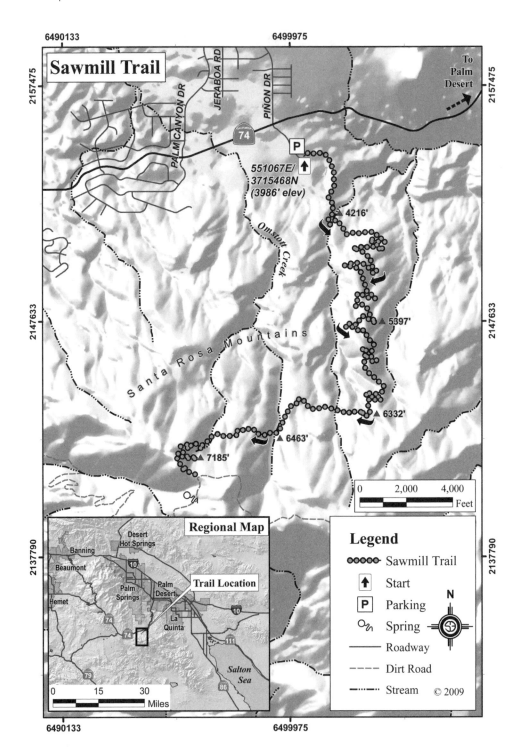

Sawmill Trail

6490133

6499975

2157475

JERABOA RD

PALM CANYON DR

PIÑON DR

To Palm Desert

74

P

551067E/
3715468N
(3986' elev)

Omstott Creek

▲ 4216'

▲ 5397'

S a n t a   R o s a   M o u n t a i n s

2147633

▲ 6332'

▲ 6463'

▲ 7185'

A

0   2,000   4,000
Feet

2137790

Regional Map

Desert Hot Springs

Banning

Beaumont

Palm Springs

Palm Desert

Trail Location

Hemet

La Quinta

74

79

111

10

10

Salton Sea

86

0   15   30
Miles

Legend

●●●●● Sawmill Trail

↑ Start

P Parking

Spring

Roadway

Dirt Road

Stream

N

© 2009

6490133

6499975

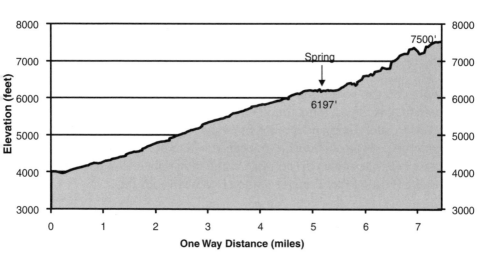

Sawmill Road Trail is the only access to the north-facing slope of the Santa Rosa Mountains and Toro Peak. You can quickly climb from the warmer Pinyon Flat area to the cooler pine-covered mountains above. The view north to the San Jacinto Mountains and surrounding areas is spectacular and it can sometimes be 25-30 degrees cooler at the top. But with an average grade of 8% this ride is best described as a strenuous aerobic workout. Technically the Sawmill Trail is a connector trail from Mount Santa Rosa Road to Sawmill Road Trail. But the ride described here combines Sawmill Road Trail and Sawmill Trail.

From the parking area follow the road as it switchbacks up the slope. When you need to catch your breath turn around and take in the beautiful views to the north. The road is rutted and washed out in places, which make it more fun than riding your average dirt road. Note that four-wheel drive vehicles, horses, and hikers take this trail, so yield the right of way.

After about 5 miles the chaparral and cactus begins to shift to pine trees. Soon you will see a kiln-like structure. This is a great place to turnaround if you have reached your aerobic limit since the next couple of miles on the Sawmill Trail connector are more strenuous and there are several downed trees to negotiate and tight switchbacks.

To keep going, turn right near the kiln structure and follow a rocky road through several ups and downs, then turn and follow it left. The road turns into a trail and soon you pass by a nice shady spot with a creek flowing by. The trail keeps climbing and several downed trees will make you get off your bike and walk around them. At long last you will reach Mount Santa Rosa Road. Water and a few picnic tables are available at Santa Rosa Spring a short distance down Mount Santa Rosa Road.

From here you can return the way you came or turn left and head toward Toro Peak area to make this a long, tough ride. The summit of Toro Peak is on private Indian Reservation land and should be respected and not climbed. The views from near the peak are wonderful. You can also turn right and follow Mount Santa Rosa Road 9 miles down to Highway 74 and then right on the pavement for 5.3 miles to the Pinyon Flats Transfer Station Road and your car.

GETTING THERE

From the junction of Highway 111 and Highway 74 in Palm Desert drive 15.6 miles and turn south on the Pinyon Flats Transfer Station Road to the Sawmill trailhead parking lot on the left side of the road. Note that you need a Forest Adventure Pass to park here.

If you're coming from the I-15 area take the Highway 79 South exit in Temecula and drive 17.5 miles to Highway 371 in Aguanga and turn north. When you reach Highway 74 in 20.5 miles turn right and drive 7.5 miles to the Pinyon Flats Transfer Station Road. Turn right to the Sawmill trailhead parking lot on the left side of the road. Note that you need a Forest Adventure Pass to park here.

OPTIONS

This ride can be combined with the Mount Santa Rosa Road ride to form a loop instead of an up and back. You can ride up Mount Santa Rosa Road and then down Sawmill. Check that ride for details and distances for Mount Santa Rosa Road. If you choose this option, it may be best to do a car shuttle, parking one car at the start of Santa Rosa Road and one at the Sawmill trailhead across from Pinyon Flat Campground (see the Mount Santa Rosa Road ride for directions). Otherwise you will have to climb 5.3 miles on busy Highway 74 to start the ride.

AMENITIES

Paradise Corner Café is a nice place to eat after the ride at the junction of Highway 74 and Highway 371. Water is available at the Pinyon Flat Campground and at Santa Rosa Spring a short distance down Mount Santa Rosa Road past the junction of Sawmill Trail if you ride that far.

Camping is available on the trail in several spots and at Hurkey Creek Park four miles southeast of Mountain Center on Highway 74. Pinyon Flat Campground is on Highway 74 at Pinyon Drive just across from the start of this ride. A number of primitive campgrounds at yellow post sites are also available off of Apple Canyon Road, on Thomas Mountain Ridge, and in the Garner Valley area and require a Forest Adventure Pass.

Trip M4 - Mount Santa Rosa Road

Starting Point	Santa Rosa Road, Highway 74
Distance	26 miles out and back (optional exit via Sawmill Trail)
Elevation Gain/Loss	5150'/1110' (one way) – 6% average grade
Riding Time	4–5 hours
Difficulty	Difficult, not technical (Sawmill exit is Strenuous, technical)
Road Conditions	Dirt road
Season	Late spring, summer, early fall
Equipment	Mountain bike
Optional Topo Map	Toro Peak, CA

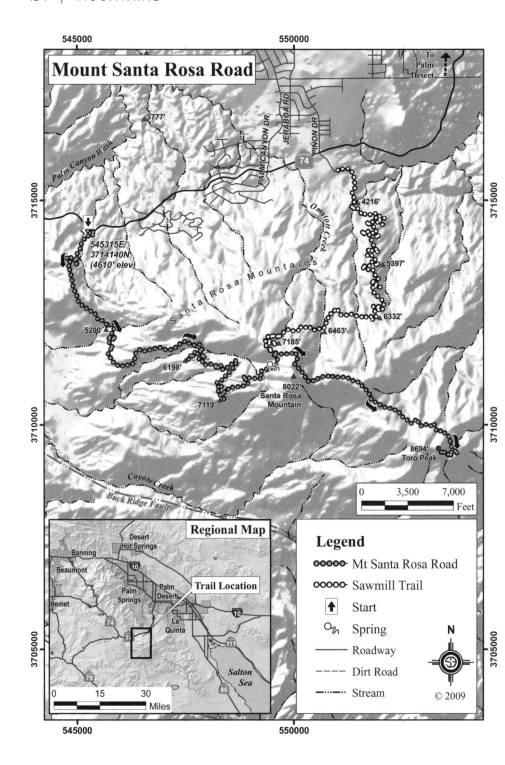

Mount Santa Rosa Road

To Palm Desert

545000
550000

3715000

3777'

PALM CANYON DR
JERABOA RD
PINON DR

74

Omstott Creek

4216'

545315E/
3714140N
(4610' elev)

5397'

Palm Canyon Wash

Santa Rosa Mountains

5200'

6332'

6463'

7185'

6198'

8022'
Santa Rosa
Mountain

7119'

8694'
Toro Peak

3710000

Coyote Creek

Buck Ridge Fault

0   3,500   7,000

Feet

Regional Map

Desert
Hot Springs

Banning

Beaumont

10

Palm
Desert

Trail Location

Hemet

74

Palm
Springs

La
Quinta

10

11

79

Salton
Sea

86

0   15   30

Miles

Legend

○●●●○— Mt Santa Rosa Road

○○○○○— Sawmill Trail

⬆ Start

○ᶜᶰ Spring

—— Roadway

- - - - Dirt Road

-··-··- Stream

N

© 2009

3705000

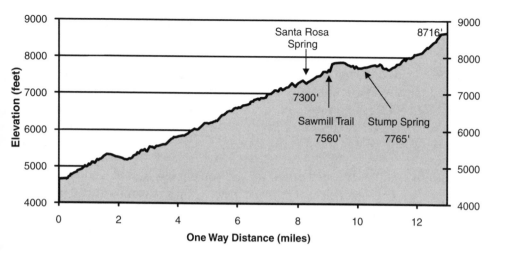

During the hot summer months in Coachella Valley the Santa Rosa Mountains beckon with spectacular vistas and dramatically cooler temperatures (the day we did the climb it was in the low 90s below and high 60s amongst the trees and sky, truly a safe haven from the busy city and stifling heat). The ride starts at 4600 feet and climbs through several vegetation zones on its way to the 8716 foot Toro Peak. The peak area offers wonderful views north to the San Jacinto and San Gorgonio Mountains and south to Anza-Borrego and mountains beyond.

In the late spring or early fall the weather can be unpredictable so dress in layers. You may even find snow near the peak. Be aware that vehicles are allowed on this road so be careful on your quick descent.

The road initially starts climbing but at mile 1.6 it levels out and actually heads somewhat downhill until mile 3 where you start the pretty consistent uphill climb. At mile 5 the chaparral starts to change to oak trees and a few pine trees. The road crosses over a small creek and then continues climbing. There are more pines as you climb and some great views south and then west into the Anza Valley area.

At 8.5 miles thankfully you can take a break by turning left at the Santa Rosa Spring sign. Some picnic tables and a good tasting spring to fill your bottles are nearby.

At 9 miles you pass a road to your left with a cable that is not attached. 20 feet beyond is a brown trail marker on your left, 5E03, that unceremoniously marks the start of the Sawmill Trail. An option for this ride is to follow the Sawmill Trail down to Highway 74. See Options below.

If you've decided to continue to the peak area, stay straight. In less than a mile the road forks with the right fork climbing slightly and curving back west. This climbs to Santa Rosa Summit where "Desert Steve" Ragsdale had a cabin. Only the foundation is left. You will see some of Desert Steve's artwork on a few trees and rocks as you continue left at the fork.

After almost 11 miles the area opens up and you pass by Stump Springs area and campground. There is a picnic table and ample place to camp. At 11.5 miles you reach another fork. Stay right and you start climbing more steeply toward the Toro Peak area. The summit of Toro Peak is on private Indian Reservation land and should be respected and not climbed. The views from near the peak are wonderful. From the Salton Sea to the east and south into Anza-Borrego Desert and the Laguna and Cuyamaca Mountains beyond that. To the north the San Jacinto and San Gorgonio Mountains rise above the desert floor.

The views are stunning, but remember to save enough time for your downhill blast. It may have taken 3-4 hours to climb but happily maybe only an hour to descend.

GETTING THERE

From the junction of Highway 111 and Highway 74 in Palm Desert drive 20 miles to Santa Rosa Road. Turn left and park here. There are a few other turnouts farther up the highway if other cars are parked here. If you're coming from the I-15 area take the Highway 79 South exit in Temecula and drive 17.5 miles to Highway 371 in Aguanga and turn north. When you reach Highway 74 in 20.5 miles turn right and drive 3.5 miles to Santa Rosa Road. Note that you need a Forest Adventure Pass to park here.

OPTIONS

This ride can be combined with the Sawmill Trail ride to form a loop instead of an up and back. Be sure to check the Sawmill Trail ride for the description and difficulty as some sections are technical. If you choose this option, it may be best to do a car shuttle, parking one car at the start of Santa Rosa Road and one at the Sawmill trailhead across from Pinyon Flat Campground (see the Sawmill Trail ride for directions). Otherwise you will have to climb 5.3 miles on Highway 74 to return to your car.

There are several places to camp on the route to the peak so another option is to share riding and driving and spend the night among the pines.

AMENITIES

Paradise Corner Café is a nice place to eat after the ride at the junction of Highway 74 and Highway 371. Water and restrooms are available at the Pinyon Flat Campground.

Camping is available on the trail in several spots and at Hurkey Creek Park four miles southeast of Mountain Center on Highway 74. Pinyon Flat Campground is on Highway 74 at Pinyon Drive 8.8 miles from the junction of Highway 371 or 15.5 miles from Highway 111 in Palm Desert. A number of primitive campgrounds at yellow post sites are also available off of Apple Canyon Road, on Thomas Mountain Ridge, and in the Garner Valley area and require a Forest Adventure Pass.

Trip M5 - Thomas Mountain Loop

Starting Point	Highway 74, Garner Valley
Distance	21 miles: 15 dirt, 6 paved
Elevation Gain/Loss	2300'/2300' – 4 % average grade
Riding Time	5 hours
Difficulty	Difficult, some technical
Road Conditions	Dirt road, paved road
Season	Spring, summer and fall as snow permits
Equipment	Mountain bike
Optional Topo Map	Anza, Idyllwild CA

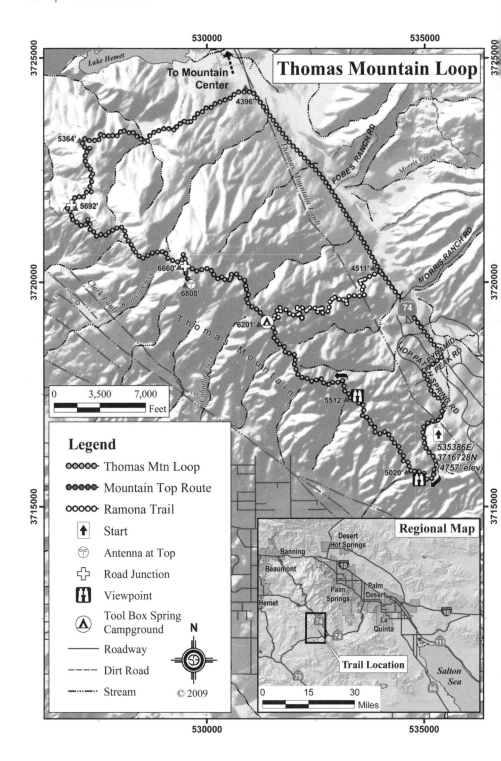

Thomas Mountain Loop

Legend

○○○○○ Thomas Mtn Loop
●●●●● Mountain Top Route
○○○○○ Ramona Trail

⬆ Start
⊕ Antenna at Top
✚ Road Junction
🔲 Viewpoint
Ⓐ Tool Box Spring
    Campground
── Roadway
---- Dirt Road
-··-··- Stream   © 2009

Regional Map

Desert Hot Springs
Banning
Beaumont
Palm Desert
Palm Springs
Hemet
La Quinta
Salton Sea

Trail Location

0   15   30
Miles

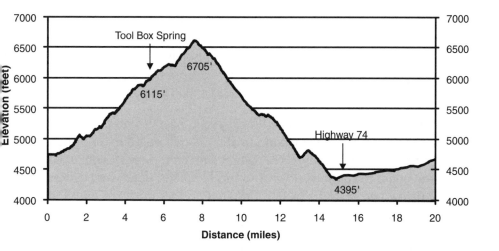

Thomas Mountain is located in the beautiful San Bernardino Mountains near Lake Hemet and Garner Valley. This is a fun ride along a forest service road that provides great scenic views of the Anza Valley to the west and the San Jacinto ridgeline to the north. There are several variations for this ride so you can make it a different ride each time you ride. The primary route outlined here starts at the south end of Thomas Mountain Road near the junction of Pyramid Peak Road and Highway 74. Other variations are described in Options below.

From the start on Hop Patch Springs Road begin riding on the dirt Thomas Mountain Road. The road climbs a fairly constant 4% grade starting in a pine tree forest and slowly changing to ribbonwood trees and chaparral as you climb. In a little over a mile a short road climbs left up a small rise. The view from the top of the rise to the Anza Valley below is spectacular. Continue back on the main road and when you reach a small spur to the right check out the great view north to the San Jacinto ridgeline and the Desert Divide to the northeast.

The road continues climbing for the next few miles and winds its way back and forth along the ridge providing alternating views west to Anza Valley and north to the San Jacinto ridgeline. Near 5.5 miles pine trees begin to appear again and the road flattens out. Tool Box Springs campground soon will be on your right. This is a nice place to rest and catch your breath. The Ramona Trail is also an optional way down from here to Highway 74 but more technical than continuing on Thomas Mountain Road and not detailed in this ride.

The next couple of miles you pass by a number of primitive yellow post campsites that make great places to spend the night if you are prepared. The road begins to climb again and at 7.5 miles a sign for 6S13C heading to the left provides a nice 0.5 mile climb to the top of the ridge. There are great views and a large antenna and the foundations of an old building. This is also a great place to camp.

Continuing on the main road the climbing is all past you now. The road starts a great downhill run at an average grade of 5%. Another 2.5 miles brings you to a junction from the left that heads in several directions. Stay straight ahead across the cattle guard to continue down Thomas Mountain Road. Great views of Lake Hemet below and the San Jacinto ridgeline to the north are found at various places along the descent.

Around 15 miles you reach Highway 74. Turn right and ride on the pavement for 6 miles back to Pyramid Peak Road passing the trailhead for the Ramona Trail on your right at 3 miles. At Pyramid Peak Road turn right, then left on Hop Patch Springs Road to return to your car.

OPTIONS

Another popular route is to start at the northern end of Thomas Mountain Road where it intersects Highway 74 near Lake Hemet and ride up, bearing left at the junction where you cross the cattle guard. Follow that to Tool Box Spring and take the Ramona Trail down to Highway 74 then left back to your car. You could also park at the Ramona Trail junction with Highway 74 and take the pavement north to Thomas Mountain Road.

GETTING THERE

From San Diego

Take I-15 to Highway 79 South and follow it east to Aguanga. Turn left on Highway 371 and continue through Anza (watch the speed limit through this area). The road starts climbing into the mountains. Turn left at Highway 74 at the Paradise Corner Café. Drive 3 miles to Pyramid Peak Road and turn left. At a T intersection turn left onto Hop Patch Springs Road and follow that 0.8 mile to where the road turns to dirt. Park on the side of the road in this area.

From Palm Spring area

From Highway 111 head south on Highway 74 for 24 miles to the junction with Highway 371. Stay on Highway 74 for 3 more miles to Pyramid Peak Road and turn left. At a T intersection turn left onto Hop Patch Springs Road and follow that 0.8 mile to where the road turns to dirt. Park on the side of the road in this area.

From Hemet

From Hemet take Highway 74 past Mountain Center and Hurkey Park. Continue past Hemet Lake Road 6 miles to Pyramid Peak Road and turn left. At a T intersection turn left onto Hop Patch Springs Road and follow that 0.8 mile to where the road turns to dirt. Park on the side of the road in this area.

AMENITIES

Paradise Corner Café is a nice place to eat after the ride at the junction of Highway 74 and Highway 371, 951-659-0730.

Camping is available at Hurkey Creek Park four miles southeast of Mountain Center on Highway 74. Pinyon Flat Campground is on Highway 74 at Pinyon Drive 8.8 miles from the junction of Highway 371 or 15.5 miles from Highway 111 in Palm Desert. A number of primitive campgrounds at yellow post sites are also available off of Apple Canyon Road, on Thomas Mountain Ridge, and in the Garner Valley area and require a Forest Adventure Pass.

Trip M6 - Morris Ranch Road

Starting Point	Highway 74, Garner Valley
Distance	8 miles out and back
Elevation Gain/Loss	1060'/150' (one way)
	7.5% grade first 2 miles, 2–3% remainder
Riding Time	1.5 hours
Difficulty	Moderate, not technical
Road Conditions	Paved road
Season	Spring, summer and fall as snow permits
Equipment	Any bike
Optional Topo Maps	Anza, Palm View Peak CA

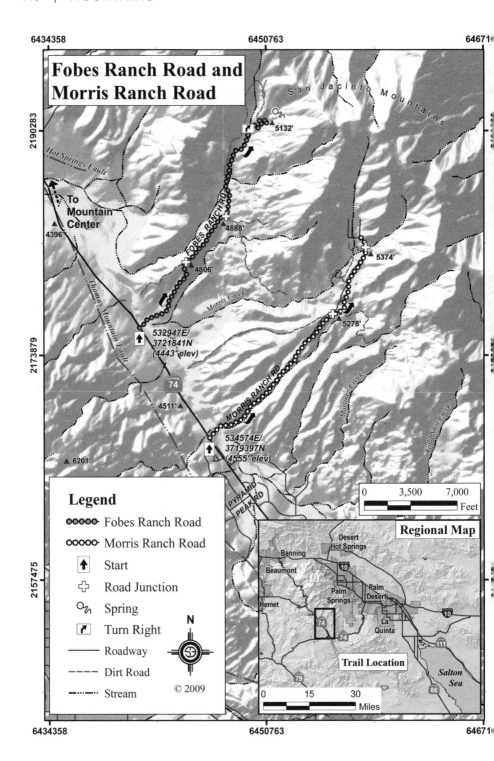

Fobes Ranch Road and Morris Ranch Road

San Jacinto Mountains

Hot Springs Fault

5132'

To Mountain Center
4396'

FOBES RANCH RD

4888'

4806'

5374'

Morris Creek

5278'

Thomas Mountain Fault

532947E/
3721841N
(4443' elev)

74

4511'

MORRIS RANCH RD

Martinez Creek

Gold Shot Creek

534574E/
3719397N
(4555' elev)

6201'

PYRAMID PEAK RD

Legend

◦◦◦◦◦ Fobes Ranch Road

◦◦◦◦◦ Morris Ranch Road

↑ Start

✚ Road Junction

◦⌐ Spring

↱ Turn Right

—— Roadway

- - - - Dirt Road

·····— Stream

N

© 2009

0   3,500   7,000
Feet

Regional Map

Desert Hot Springs

Banning

Beaumont

10

Palm Springs

Palm Desert

Hemet

74

La Quinta

10

79

111

Trail Location

Salton Sea

86

0   15   30
Miles

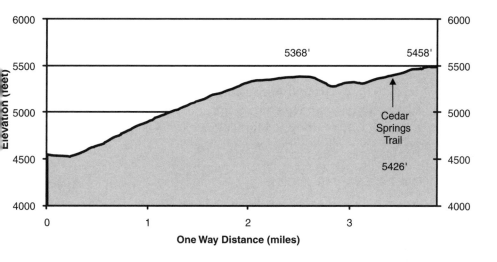

Like the Fobes Ranch Road ride, this ride also begins in beautiful Garner Valley in the quiet San Jacinto Mountains. The Garner Valley is dominated by grasslands with stands of mainly ponderosa pine. Fobes Ranch Road climbs its way northeast toward the Desert Divide and Spitler Peak providing wonderful views of the San Jacinto Mountains to the north and east, the Santa Rosa Mountains to the south, and Thomas Mountain to the southwest. The Desert Divide is the lower section of the San Jacinto Mountain chain that is part of the San Bernardino National Forest.

The road starts out downhill from the fire station, crosses over a wash and passes the forest service station where it begins a fairly steady 7.5% climb along a small canyon with oak and pine trees. At 2 miles the road begins to level out across a ridge dominated by chaparral. There are nice views of the Desert Divide and surrounding mountains from here. At 3.6 miles you pass the Cedar Springs Trail on your right.

At 2.75 miles you enjoy a small downhill run and then more steeply downhill. The road rolls up and down the remainder of the way. When the road ends at two private roads heading left and right, turn around and enjoy the nice downhill ride back to your starting point.

GETTING THERE

From San Diego

Take I-15 to Highway 79 South and follow it east to Aguanga. Turn left on Highway 371 and continue through Anza (watch the speed limit through this area). The road starts climbing into the mountains. Turn left at Highway 74 at the Paradise Corner Café. Drive 4 miles to Morris Ranch Road and park off the road near the intersection. You will see the Garner Valley Fire Station on the right.

From Palm Springs area

From Highway 111 head south on Highway 74 for 24 miles to the junction with Highway 371. Stay on Highway 74 for 4 more miles to Morris Ranch Road and park off the road near the intersection. You will see the Garner Valley Fire Station on the right.

From Hemet

From Hemet take Highway 74 past Mountain Center and Hurkey Park. Continue past Hemet Lake Road 4 miles to Morris Ranch Road and park off the road near the intersection. You will see the Garner Valley Fire Station on the right.

AMENITIES

Paradise Corner Café is a nice place to eat after the ride at the junction of Highway 74 and Highway 371, 951-659-0730.

Camping is available at Hurkey Creek Park 4 miles southeast of Mountain Center on Highway 74. Pinyon Flat Campground is on Highway 74 at Pinyon Drive 8.8 miles from the junction of Highway 371 or 15.5 miles from Highway 111 in Palm Desert. A number of primitive campgrounds at yellow post sites are also available off of Apple Canyon Road, on Thomas Mountain Ridge, and in the Garner Valley area and require a Forest Adventure Pass.

Trip M7 - Fobes Ranch Road

Starting Point	Garner Valley, Highway 74
Distance	8 miles out and back
Elevation Gain/Loss	1000'/140' (one way) 4% average grade, 9% in a couple spots
Riding Time	2 hours
Difficulty	Moderate, not technical
Road Conditions	Dirt road
Season	Spring, summer and fall as snow permits
Equipment	Mountain bike
Optional Topo Maps	Idyllwild, Palm View Peak CA

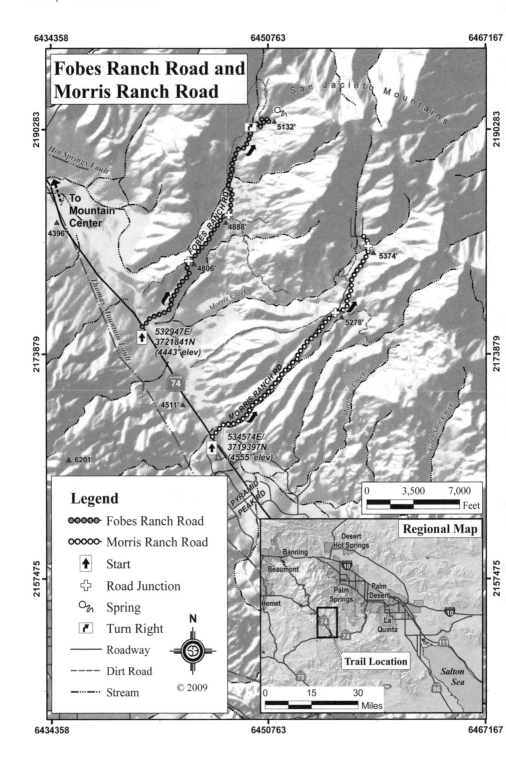

Fobes Ranch Road and Morris Ranch Road

San Jacinto Mountains

Hot Springs Fault

To Mountain Center
4396'

5132'

4888'

4806'

Morris Creek

5374'

5278'

532947E/
3721841N
(4443' elev)

Thomas Mountain Fault

74

4511'

Martinez Creek

Gold Shot Creek

6201'

534574E/
3719397N
(4555' elev)

PYRAMID PEAK RD

Legend
- ●○○○○ Fobes Ranch Road
- ○○○○○ Morris Ranch Road
- ⬆ Start
- ✛ Road Junction
- ☌ Spring
- ↱ Turn Right
- ⸻ Roadway
- ---- Dirt Road
- ····· Stream

N

© 2009

0   3,500   7,000
Feet

Regional Map

Desert Hot Springs

Banning

Beaumont

10

Palm Desert

Palm Springs

Hemet

La Quinta

10

111

Trail Location

Salton Sea

79

86

0   15   30
Miles

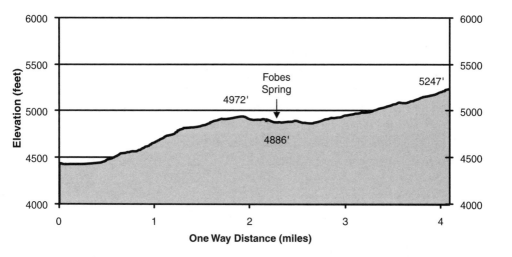

Garner Valley is a beautiful high mountain valley in the San Jacinto Mountains away from the noise and traffic in nearby Hemet, Idyllwild, and Palm Springs. Fobes Ranch Road starts in the scenic Garner Valley, dominated by grasslands with stands of mainly ponderosa pine. The road climbs its way northeast toward the Desert Divide, providing wonderful views of the San Jacinto Mountains to the north and east, the Santa Rosa Mountains to the south and Thomas Mountain to the southwest. The ride described here is a simple out and back but you can venture on some of the side roads and make loops of various lengths.

Start riding east and at 0.4 mile stay left at the junction. There are many trails winding through the trees to the right that are not covered here. The road starts climbing rather quickly up a ridge. At 1.2 miles the slope lets up a bit and you get a chance to enjoy the beautiful views. A road intersects from the left near here. Although not covered here this road leads back down another ridge.

At 1.75 miles the climb eases up again and heads across the top of a hill for about 0.5 miles. The road then drops a bit and starts climbing again. At 3.5 miles stay right at the signed junction indicating the Fobes Trail is 0.5 and Pacific Crest Trail 2 miles ahead. Once the trail start to curve left in some trees the end of the road is just ahead blocked by a gate. Turn around at this point and return the way you came.

GETTING THERE

From San Diego

Take I-15 to Highway 79 South and follow it east to Aguanga. Turn left on Highway 371 and continue through Anza (watch the speed limit through this area). The road starts climbing into the mountains. Turn left at Highway 74 at the Paradise Corner Café. Drive 7.5 miles to Fobes Ranch Road, 6S05, just past mile marker 66.25. Turn right drive a little ways and park off the road here. A Forest Adventure Pass may be needed here.

From Palm Springs area

From Highway 111 head south on Highway 74 for 24 miles to the junction with Highway 371. Stay on Highway 74 for 5.8 miles to Fobes Ranch Road, 6S05, just past mile marker 66.25. Turn right drive a little ways and park off the road here. A Forest Adventure Pass may be needed here.

From Hemet

From Hemet take Highway 74 past Mountain Center and Hurkey Park. Continue past Hemet Lake Road 2.2 miles to Fobes Ranch Road, 6S05, just past mile marker 66. Turn right drive a little ways and park off the road here. A Forest Adventure Pass may be needed here.

AMENITIES

Paradise Corner Café is a nice place to eat after the ride at the junction of Highway 74 and Highway 371, 951-659-0730.

Camping is available at Hurkey Creek Park four miles southeast of Mountain Center on Highway 74. Pinyon Flat Campground is on Highway 74 at Pinyon Drive 8.8 miles from the junction of Highway 371 or 15.5 miles from Highway 111 in Palm Desert. A number of primitive campgrounds at yellow post sites are also available off of Apple Canyon Road, on Thomas Mountain Ridge, and in the Garner Valley area and require a Forest Adventure Pass.

Trip M8 - Apple Canyon Road

Starting Point	Highway 74, Mountain Center
Distance	6 miles out and back
Elevation Gain/Loss	706'/60' (one way) – 5 % grade
Riding Time	1.5 hours
Difficulty	Moderate, not technical
Road Conditions	Paved road
Season	Spring, summer and fall as snow permits
Equipment	Any bike
Optional Topo Map	Idyllwild, CA

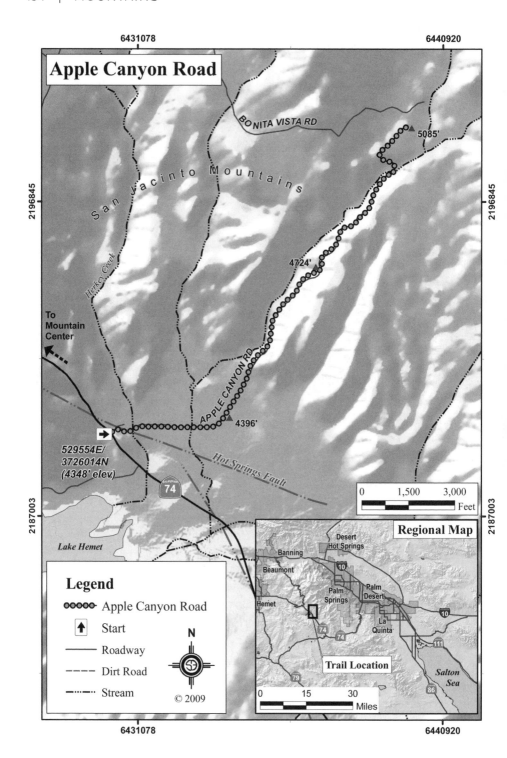

Apple Canyon Road

6431078

6440920

BONITA VISTA RD

5085'

San Jacinto Mountains

Herkey Creek

4724'

To
Mountain
Center

APPLE CANYON RD

4396'

Start

529554E/
3726014N
(4348' elev)

Hot Springs Fault

CALIFORNIA
74

Lake Hemet

0   1,500   3,000
Feet

Legend

ooooo Apple Canyon Road

⬆ Start

—— Roadway

- - - Dirt Road

-··-·· Stream

N

© 2009

Regional Map

Desert
Hot Springs

Banning

Beaumont

10

Palm
Springs

Palm
Desert

Hemet

La
Quinta

111

10

74

74

Trail Location

Salton
Sea

79

86

0   15   30
Miles

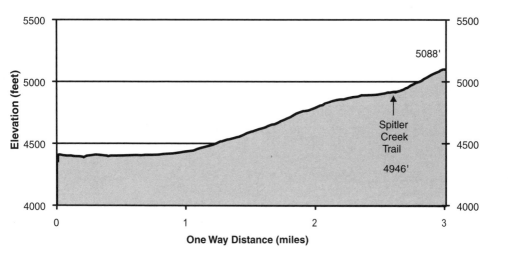

Apple Canyon Road begins near Lake Hemet and Hurkey Creek Park in the scenic Garner Valley and climbs toward the Desert Divide, the lower section of the San Jacinto Mountain chain that is part of the San Bernardino National Forest. The Pacific Crest Trail follows the Desert Divide above Apple Canyon. Wonderful views of the San Jacinto Mountains to the north, the Santa Rosa Mountains to the south, Thomas Mountain to the southwest, and Lake Hemet are visible in places on this ride.

The road starts out slightly downhill, levels out and then starts slowly climbing around 1 mile. Soon you pass dirt roads leading to yellow stake primitive campgrounds among the sweet-smelling pine trees.

There are nice views of the surrounding mountains from here. At 2.5 miles is a dirt parking area and soon the trailhead for Spitler Creek Trail, 3E22 indicating the Pacific Crest Trail is 5 miles up. Bikes are not allowed on this trail.

At 2.75 miles you enjoy a small downhill run and then the road rolls up and down the remainder of the way through the beautiful valley. When the road ends turn around and enjoy the nice downhill ride back to your starting point watching for views of Lake Hemet as you descend.

GETTING THERE

From San Diego

Take I-15 to Highway 79 South and follow it east to Aguanga. Turn left on Highway 371 and continue through Anza (watch the speed limit through this area). The road starts climbing into the mountains. Turn left at Highway 74 at the Paradise Corner Café. Drive 9.3 miles to Apple Canyon Road and park off the road near here.

From Palm Spring area

From Highway 111 head south on Highway 74 for 24 miles to the junction with Highway 371. Stay on Highway 74 for 9.3 more miles to Apple Canyon Road and park off the road near here.

From Hemet

From Hemet take Highway 74 past Mountain Center and turn left at Apple Canyon Road and Hurkey Park and park off the road near here.

AMENITIES

Paradise Corner Café is a nice place to eat after the ride at the junction of Highway 74 and Highway 371, 951-659-0730.

Camping is available at Hurkey Creek Park at the turnoff to Apple Canyon Road. Pinyon Flat Campground is on Highway 74 at Pinyon Drive 8.8 miles from the junction of Highway 371 or 15.5 miles from Highway 111 in Palm Desert. A number of primitive campgrounds at yellow post sites are also available off of Apple Canyon Road, on Thomas Mountain ridge, and in the Garner Valley area and require a Forest Adventure Pass.

Appendix 1

Rides by Difficulty

EASY RIDES

Number	Name	Distance (miles)	Time	Elevation Gain/Loss
W2	Palm Springs City Loop	2.5	30 min	50'50'
W4	Deepwell Tour	2.5	30 min	50'/50'
E5	Terra Lago Tour	3 or 4.5	30 min	Flat
E3	**Cove Oasis Trails**	**2–5**	**30–60 min**	**100'/100'**
E4	Indio Mural Tour	4	45 min	Flat
W5	Canyon Country Club Route	5	45 min	75'/75'
W7	Tahquitz Creek Tour	5	45 min	75'/75'
E1	Bear Creek Trail	5.5	45 min	350'/350'
C1	Rancho Mirage Scenic Tour	7	45 min	100'/100'
M1	**Pinyon Flat Ride**	**6**	**1.5 hr**	**540'/540'**
W3	Palm Springs City Wide Loop	11	1 hr	250'/250'
W9	Cathedral City Tour	12	1 hr	50'/200' ow
E9	Box Canyon Earthquake Route	24	1.5 hr	20'/1900'

MODERATE RIDES

Number	Name	Distance (miles)	Time	Elevation Gain/Loss	Technical Difficulty
C8	Randall Henderson Trail	5	1.5 hr	400'/400'	Slightly
E7	Little Box Canyon Trail	6	1.5 hr	300'/300'	
W6	South Palm Canyon Ride	7 or 10	1–1.5 hr	370'/370'	
C3	Cahuilla Hills "Cowboy" Trails	1.5 – 3.5	1–1.5 hr	1000'/1000'	Slightly
M8	Apple Canyon Road	6	1.5 hr	706'/60' ow	
M6	Morris Ranch Road	8	1.5 hr	1060'/150' ow	
M7	Fobes Ranch Road	8	2 hr	1000'/140' ow	
E6	Painted Canyon	9	2.5 hr	600'/40' ow	
E8	Meccacopia Trail	11	3–4 hr	220'/1180'	
C5	Living Desert Hill Climb	19	1.5–2 hr	900'/900'	
W8	Goat Trails	3 – 5	2–3 hr	600'/100' ow	Slightly
C7	Palm Desert and La Quinta Loop	40, 33, or 20	2–3.5 hr	760'/760'	
E2	La Quinta Loop	24	2 hr	400'/400'	

DIFFICULT RIDES

Number	Name	Distance (miles)	Time	Elevation Gain/Loss	Technical Difficulty
C2	Bump and Grind Trail	4.5	2 hr	1300'/320' ow	Slightly
W1	Tram Road Ride	8	90+ min	2150'/2150'	
M5	Thomas Mountain Loop	21	5 hr	2300'/2300'	Some
M4	Mount Santa Rosa Road	26	4–5 hr	5150'/1110' ow	
C6	Coachella Valley Preserve and Dillon Road Ride	48	4 hr	1550'/1550'	
M2	Palm Canyon – Pinyon Flat Loop	11	3.5 hr	2300'/2300'	Technical

STRENUOUS RIDES

Number	Name	Distance (miles)	Time	Elevation Gain/Loss	Technical Difficulty
C4	Hopalong Cassidy Trail	10	3 hr	3060'/3170' ow	Technical
M3	Sawmill Trail	16	4–5 hr	3850'/3850'	Technical
C9	Art Smith Trail	16	5–6 hr	2670'1310' ow	Some

Notes:

Bold rides are mountain bike rides

In Elevation Gain/Loss "ow" means one way measurement. Reverse these numbers for the return route.

Appendix 2

References and Suggested Reading

Cornett, James W., *Wonders of the Coachella Valley*, 2008, Nature Trails Press

Ferranti, Philip, *120 Great Hikes in and near Palm Springs*, 2003, Westcliffe Publishers

Fragnoli, Delaine and Douglass Don, *Mountain Biking Southern California's Best 100 Trails*, 1998, Mountain Biking Press

Niemann, Greg, *Palm Springs Legends: Creation of a Desert Oasis*, 2006, Sunbelt Publications

Pyle, Linda McMillan, *Peaks, Palms & Picnics*, 2002, Sunbelt Publications

Palm Springs Life, Palm Springs: Desert Publications, Milton Jones, publisher. *http://www.palmspringslife.com/*

Appendix 2

Recommended Companions from the Sunbelt Bookshelf
"Adventures in the Natural History and Cultural Heritage of the Californias"

Palm Springs Legends: Creation of a Desert Oasis   Greg Niemann
From the Land of the Cahuilla to the Legacy of Indian Canyons, 50 fascinating vignettes portray
this storied land.

Gold and Silver in the Mojave: Images of a Last Frontier   Nicholas Clapp
"The glamour, grit, gold, and grandeur of the desert" on Coachella Valley's northern ramparts.

Baja California Plant Field Guide SDNHM   Jon Rebman & Norm Roberts
Over 50% of this updated full-color classic applies also to the desert & highlands of southern
California.

Desert Legends and Lore of California's Colorado and Mojave Deserts   Choral Pepper
Lost mines, Indian myths, legendary characters, strange natural features, and fabled treasure ships.

Afoot & Afield Inland Empire: A Comprehensive Hiking Guide   David & Jennifer Money Harris
75 trails in the Coachella Valley and surrounding mountains of the Santa Rosas, San Jacintos, &
Joshua Tree National Park.

Palm Springs Oasis: A Portfolio of the Coachella Valley Region   Greg Lawson
A treasured photographic memory of landscapes, creatures, and natural beauty of this famed desert
paradise.

Peaks, Palms, and Picnics: Day Journeys in the Coachella Valley   Linda Pyle
Itineraries for walks, hikes, visitor centers. and parks; fun for kids of any age with a special culi-
nary treat for each of the 31 adventures.

Wonders of the Coachella Valley: A Nature Guide   James W. Cornett
10 trips describing the Valley's natural lore of climate, geology, wildlife, and Native Americans.

140 Great Hikes in and near Palm Springs   Philip Ferante
Exciting outdoor excursions for hikers of ages and skill by the area's best-known hiking guru.

Day & Overnight Hikes, Palm Springs   Laura Randall
GPS-based trail maps & elevation profiles with directions to the trailheads & descriptions of 32 of
Palm Springs' outstanding trails.

San Jacinto Wilderness Trail Map and San Gorgonio Wilderness Map   Tom Harrison
Two "must-haves" for this region from California's finest and most essential map series.

Cycling the Palm Springs Region   Nelson Copp & Margaret Gooding
35 route descriptions and superb maps in the Coachella Valley & surrounding mountains. From the
same authors: *Cycling San Diego* and *Cycling the Trails of San Diego*.

Sunbelt books celebrate the land and its people through publications in
natural science, outdoor adventure, history, regional literature, and references.

www.sunbeltbook.com
9/2013

Appendix 3

Coachella Valley Cyclist's Directory

GROUPS, CLUBS, AND RIDES

California Bicycle Coalition
http://www.calbike.org/

Coachella Valley Hiking Club
http://cvhikingclub.net/

Community Trails Alliance
http://www.cvcta.org

Desert Bicycle Club
http://www.cycleclub.com/

Desert Trails Hiking Club
http://www.deserttrailshiking.com

Friends of the Desert Mountains
http://www.desertmountains.org/

International Mountain Biking Association
http://www.imba.com/

Sun City Palm Desert Cyclists
http://desertcyclists.homestead.com/

Tour de Palm Springs
http://www.tourdepalmsprings.com/sponsors.htm

GEOLOGY AND CONSERVATION

BLM Santa Rosa and San Jacinto Mountains National Monument
http://www.blm.gov/ca/st/en/fo/palmsprings/santarosa.html

Coachella Valley Multiple Species Habitat Conservation Plan
http://www.cvmshcp.org/

San Andreas Fault
http://geology.com/articles/san-andreas-fault.shtml

Santa Rosa and San Jacinto Mountains National Monument
http://www.palmspringslife.com/santarosa/

REFERENCES BY CITY OR REGION

Cathedral City

Cathedral City Home Page
http://www.cathedralcity.gov/

Indio

Clark's Travel Center Mural page
http://www.clarkstravelcenter.com/mural.html

Coachella Valley Museum and Cultural Center
http://www.coachellavalleymuseum.org/

Indio Chamber of Commerce
http://www.indiochamber.org

Indio Chamber of Commerce Mural page
http://www.indiochamber.org/murals.html

Indio Historic Route 99
http://www.indiocaroute99.com/

Shields Date Gardens
http://www.shieldsdates.com/

Terra Lago Page
http://www.terralago.com/community/

La Quinta

City of La Quinta
http://www.la-quinta.org/

La Quinta Cove Neighborhood Association
http://www.laquintacove.org/

Old Town La Quinta
http://www.oldtownlaquinta.com/

Top of the Cove Neighborhood Association
http://www.tclq.com/Home_Page.php

Mecca/Thermal

BLM Mecca Hills Wilderness
http://www.blm.gov/ca/pa/wilderness/wa/areas/mecca_hills.html

BLM Meccacopia Special Recreation Management Area
http://www.blm.gov/ca/st/en/fo/palmsprings/mecacopia_srma.html

City of Mecca
http://www.meccaca.com/

Oasis Date Gardens
http://www.oasisdate.com/

Mountains

BLM Santa Rosa and San Jacinto Mountains National Monument
http://www.blm.gov/ca/st/en/fo/palmsprings/santarosa.html

Idyllwild Life Magazine
http://www.idyllwildlife.com/

Pinyon Flat and other campgrounds
http://www.fs.fed.us/r5/sanbernardino/recreation/camping/

San Jacinto Ranger District
http://www.fs.fed.us/r5/sanbernardino/contact/sanjacinto.shtml

Santa Rosa and San Jacinto Mountains National Monument
http://www.palmspringslife.com/santarosa/

Santa Rosa and San Jacinto Mountains National Monument Visitor Center
http://www.desertmountains.org/bookstore/bookstore.html

Palm Desert

City of Palm Desert
http://www.cityofpalmdesert.org/

Hopalong Cassidy
http://www.hopalong.com/home.asp

George Francis "Gabby" Hayes
http://www.b-westerns.com/pals-gh.htm

Living Desert
http://www.livingdesert.org

Palm Desert
http://www.palm-desert.org/

Santa Rosa and San Jacinto Mountains National Monument Visitor Center
http://www.desertmountains.org/bookstore/bookstore.html

Palm Springs

City of Palm Springs
http://www.ci.palm-springs.ca.us/

Palm Springs Aerial Tramway
www.pstramway.com

Palm Springs Chamber of Commerce
http://www.pschamber.org/

Palm Springs National Golf & Country Club
http://palmspringsnationalgolfclub.com/

Ron Root's "Unofficial History" of Deepwell
http://www.asher-white.com/Deepwell_History.pdf

Walk of Stars
http://www.palmsprings.com/stars/

Rancho Mirage

City of Rancho Mirage
http://www.ci.rancho-mirage.ca.us/

Michael S. Wolfson Park
http://www.ci.rancho-mirage.ca.us/residents/things_to_do/parks_and_trails.php

Rancho Mirage Chamber of Commerce Recreation
http://www.ranchomirage.org/recreation_leisure.html

Riverside County

Chiriaco Summit
http://www.chiriacosummit.com/

Coachella Valley Preserve
http://coachellavalleypreserve.org/
http://3dparks.wr.usgs.gov/joshuatree/html/coachella.htm

General Patton Memorial Museum, Chiriaco Summit
http://www.generalpattonmuseum.com/

BIKE SHOPS AND SPORTING GOODS STORES
Idyllwild

The Bike Route bike shop
54095 Pine Crest Ave. Idyllwild, CA 92549
(951) 659-2038

Indio

Don's Bike & Skateboard Shop
81580 US Highway 111
Indio, CA
(760) 347-0119
http://www.donsbikestore.com/

La Quinta

Big Five Sporting Goods
78710 Highway 111
La Quinta, CA 92253
(760) 771-6626

Palm Desert

Bikeman
42220 Green Way
Palm Desert, CA 92211
(760) 341-5022

Palm Desert Cyclery
77-780 Country Club Drive
Palm Desert, CA 92211
(760) 345-9096
http://pscyclery.com/

Tri-A-Bike
44841 San Pablo Avenue
Palm Desert, CA 92260-3574
(760) 340-2840
http://www.triabike.com/

Big 5 Sporting Goods
72284 Highway 111
Palm Desert, CA 92260
(760) 340-3358

Palm Springs

Palm Springs Cyclery
611 S Palm Canyon Dr
Palm Springs, CA 92264-7453
(760) 325-9319
http://pscyclery.com/

Big 5 Sporting Goods
364 S Palm Canyon Dr
Palm Springs,CA 92262
(760) 325-0255

Rancho Mirage

Velo Bum Elite Cyclery
71430 Highway 111
Rancho Mirage, CA 92270
(760) 341-2463
http://www.velobum.com/

Thousand Palms

Joel's Bicycle Shop
72226 Varner Rd
Thousand Palms, CA
(760) 343-2271

Index

The main pages for each of the rides are shown in **bold**.